What Others Are Saying

"Homelessness in a country like ours is absurd. This is an important—relevant—book that should be required reading."

— **Larry King**
CNN's Larry King Live

"There is no excuse for homelessness in America. There are practical answers, and Joel John Roberts has spotlighted many of them."

— **Pat Boone**
Musician, Actor, Entertainer

"Joel has written an extremely clever and honest book on how to fix our broken system of homelessness that exists in our communities—and he well knows the problems. I highly recommend it!"

— **Rhonda Fleming**
Actress, Philanthropist

"I've been lucky to have PATH as part of the Continuum of Care to meet my goal of ending chronic homelessness in Los Angeles in ten years. PATH's nationally recognized model provides individuals and families the housing and support services they need to get back to work and make positive contributions to our society and economy."

— **James K. Hahn**
Mayor, City of Los Angeles, California

"Joel Roberts' book, *How To Increase Homelessness* is an important social treatise on one of the great failures of our society. For every caring person, the book is a must-read. Thereafter, we have to roll up our sleeves, get to work, and solve this problem."

— **Mark Egerman**
Mayor, City of Beverly Hills, California

"*How To Increase Homelessness* is a fascinating book that is very relevant for those who want to understand the challenge of homelessness confronting communities across the country. It should be required reading for anyone seeking solutions to this complex societal problem."

— **Roosevelt F. Dorn**
Mayor, City of Inglewood, California

"Joel Roberts is a true visionary on how to address issues related to homelessness and has been a great advocate and city partner with the City of West Hollywood."

— **John J. Duran**
Mayor, City of West Hollywood, California

"A common sense discussion of one of our nation's toughest - and most embarrassing – issues. This book is a must-read for all policymakers."

— **Richard Bloom**
Mayor, City of Santa Monica, California

"Joel John Roberts runs one of the country's most successful programs for those who are homeless. This book should be on the must-read list of every city council member, county supervisor, mayor, legislator and governor in the country, as well as anyone who cares for those who are less fortunate."

— **Sharon Davis**
Former First Lady of California

"Joel Roberts' insight into the phenomenon of homelessness is the kind that can only come from first hand work with the homeless. I highly recommend this book."

— **Eric Garcetti**
Los Angeles City Council Member, 13th District

"*How To Increase Homelessness* brilliantly challenges our country to completely change course in order to end homelessness. Everyone who is concerned about homelessness should read this book."

— Mitchell Netburn
Executive Director, Los Angeles Homeless Services Authority

"Joel's insights and his passion for the issues challenge us to not accept the inevitability of homelessness, and to acknowledge we all have a stake in its defeat. Joel is a charismatic visionary with practical solutions and the personal qualities needed to lead in this area of social change."

— Tessie Guillermo
President/CEO, Community Technology Foundation of California, San Francisco

"Roberts and his visionary board of directors have demonstrated that 'thinking outside of the box' results in transformation for many who arrive at PATH's front door. This book leverages PATH's impact by stimulating creative policy discussion among all of us who are frustrated with the status quo."

— Kerry Morrison
Executive Director, Hollywood Entertainment District

"Our country has become so complacent about poverty that we need Roberts' timely 'absurdist' manifesto to controvert the existing common wisdom—that homelessness is an acceptable by-product of life. Joel forces us to question this ridiculous attitude and act to correct it."

— Yancy Ruben Garrido
Innovative Philanthropy, New York City

"I can think of few social issues that generate such polarization and impasse as homelessness. In a sensible, compassionate, and fresh approach, Joel Roberts opens a pathway to challenge us all to create solutions and the will to end homelessness."

— Rhonda Meister
Executive Director, St. Joseph Center;
member of the Los Angeles Mayor's Blue Ribbon Panel on Homelessness

"Joel Roberts asks tough and overdue questions about public policy, including pressing America about whether they are content to let half of our foster children 'emancipate' to homelessness."

— Joanne R. Feldmeth
Executive Director, ChildSHARE

"This is a timely and powerful wake up call for the community to realize that if we are not working together to develop solutions to homelessness then we are part of the problem. Joel has ingeniously articulated the parameters of this complex problem in a way that enables the reader to readily visualize a long-term solution. It is a masterful work."

— Paul Freese, Jr.
Director of Litigation & Advocacy, Public Counsel

"Provocative and knowledgeable, Roberts speaks from years of experience in helping homeless people find a way to self-sufficient living. It is a 'must read' for anyone who cares about what is happening to the 'least and lost' among us."

— Rev. Charles Orr
*Senior Pastor, Westwood Presbyterian Church,
the faith group that started PATH*

"Hear Joel Roberts, for he is a prophet. His practical and relevant solutions that give hope to ending homelessness must be embraced for the situation is not a social accident. The finger points at all of us—we are indifferent. Where is our outrage?"

— Mary Erickson
Director of Urban Outreach, Bel Air Presbyterian Church

"To many of us, we see homelessness as a problem without a solution. However, Joel Roberts and PATH have demonstrated that the right strategic vision fueled by the commitment of many dedicated individuals and corporations can enable homeless people to become hopeful people."

— Dr. Kenneth Fong
Senior Pastor, Evergreen Baptist Church of Los Angeles

How to Increase Homelessness

Real Solutions to the Absurdity
of Homelessness in America

JOEL JOHN ROBERTS

LOYAL

LoyalPublishing.com

Published by Loyal Publishing, Inc., Bend, Oregon— LoyalPublishing.com
Edited by Allan Lemke

Cover design by Fresh Ink Studios: FreshInkStudios.com

Cover Art © 2004 Craig Smallish / Getty Images

Dedicated To:

Claire West Orr

A friend, mentor, and founder of PATH

To end homelessness, we need everyone's help.

This is my small contribution to the cause...   Joel

CONTENTS

Acknowledgements

Every project needs a team, and every person needs a village. This book project became a reality because of the village that supports me. "I am somebody"—as the Rev. Jesse Jackson encouraged in me at a youth rally when I was young—because people in my life invested in me.

My circle of love. My mother, Jean Roberts, who instilled in me the values that guide me. My children, Grace Joy, Justin Adam, and Stephen Christopher. And other family members, Charles Roberts Jr., Lisa and Lou Lauriano, Charley and Vicki Roberts, Kristen Brooks, Brian and Kim Roberts, Janet and Joyce Roberts, and Charlie Chang. If every person had a circle of love like mine, homelessness would not occur.

The PATH circle. Eight years ago, a group of community volunteers who were the PATH Board of Directors took a chance by hiring me as the Executive Director. I would not have been able to write this book without them. They, too, have become my friends, mentors, and personal advocates—people like, Ron and Carole Fox, Bob Shober, Terry Bird, Eva Vollmer, Michael Goldberg, Stan Schneider, Ava Fries, Denise Avchen, Aris Anagnos, and Julie Summers (I'm sure I forgot someone...) I'm also honored to work alongside a dedicated and talented staff at

PATH—including Janet Ganaway, Mousa Vorodi, and Maggie Willis who helped read the manuscript.

My circle of faith. People of faith are the ones who helped shape my leadership skills starting at an early age. My grandfather, Dr. Charles Roberts, a missionary to China. And my pastors throughout my life: Dr. George Johnson, Rev. Joe Johnson, Rev. Cory Ishida, Dr. Ken Fong, and Rev. Charles Orr. And long-time friends, Ron Byrnes, Bob Mabry and Stevens Wright.

I am also grateful to Chris Northrup, a terrific publicist who helped with the creative chapter titles and has helped shape PATH's message to the world. Matt Jacobson, my literary agent, who read my manuscript on adoption and has been advocating for me ever since. And G. Allan Kingston, CEO of Century Housing who wrote the Afterword and is a leader among leaders.

Finally, "I am somebody," because of my faith in God. God is my ultimate travel agent who has laid before me an amazing journey.

ONE

The Absurd

The picture is absurd.

Our First World urban communities filled with herds of people rushing to work, automobiles zooming on thoroughfares like a colony of ants, and storefronts bustling with commercial activity. It's a postcard picture of the success of our nation. A Kodak® moment.

But if you keep looking and focusing your eyes on the image, as if gazing into a Viewmaster® viewer, another depiction is revealed. In the gleaming reflections of the glassed-covered skyscrapers, hidden at times, lies the toll of human neglect: ragged women pushing shopping carts filled with life's possessions; men walking along sidewalks mumbling to imaginary people; decades old cars stuffed with homeless families—moms with children—huddling in the only shelter they possess.

Those "regular people" living and working in this urban village ignore this plight as if it doesn't exist. It's easy to do. The rush of commerce, the urgency of living, the priority of recreation - all conspire to overwhelm any concern for these people who don't fit into the paradigm of success. So the rushing and zooming and bustling of life continues while the plight of human neglect drudges on.

What's wrong with this picture that in reality is discolored and out-of-focus? This picture that belongs more in an old box in the attic than as a digital snapshot of   today's reality.

When you think about it, this reality is simply ridiculous. We are the richest, most powerful country in the world, perhaps in history. And yet we allow thousands and thousands of our own people to languish on the streets as if our cities strive to become Calcutta. We created the Internet, sent people to the moon, built pocket-sized telephones that need no wires. We export motion pictures that billions of people watch, create architectural monuments, develop educational institutions that the world envies, and possess a military capability that instills overwhelming fear.

And yet, look at the picture again. With all of this wealth, creativity, and might, we cannot end homelessness in our own country.

It's absurd.

Our community's response is even more ridiculous. Some people are so disgusted with the problem that they place the blame on the victims. As if it's the wife's fault that her husband is beating her up. So she ends up becoming homeless because she caused the beatings. It's the same attitude toward other people who are homeless. The homeless deserve their plight because they are incredibly lazy, raging alcoholics, mentally deranged. Why help someone who doesn't want to help himself?

And then there are those in our community who would grant the homeless excessive rights. Let the homeless urinate on the sidewalks, let them feed like animals at outdoor sites, and give them the right to sleep on dangerous streets and cold park benches.

Both extremes are absurd. There are genuine victims, so people should not have the right to live and sleep in dangerous, unhealthy conditions.

Our communities point the blaming finger at   each other:

"It's the fault of the caregivers—the social service agencies—who attract more homeless people into our neighborhoods."

"The police should be arresting homeless people because they blight our neighborhoods."

"The government should be spending more money on the problem."

"Politicians only listen to powerful business communities and neighborhood associations who vote them into office."

Local city officials argue with regional county administrators blaming each other for not providing enough funding. Wealthy developers gentrifying blighted neighborhoods are expelling the poor onto the streets for the sake of redevelopment. Round and round the blaming finger goes. Where it stops everybody knows. The fingers are pointed at one and all. From the homeless person himself to the caregivers who help. From businesses and neighborhoods who fear the affects, to the political officials who hold the purse strings.

It is a constant cycle of blame. So the creative energies, political influence, and vast resources that could be used to house the homeless are instead used to defend someone's position. The members of the community are fighting each other instead of fighting the problem.

The cycle is simply absurd.

TWO

The Absurd Conclusion

As the director of a homeless service agency, I have seen firsthand the frustration, anger, hurt, and pleas of the homeless person, the service provider, the business community, the neighborhoods, the political offices. The problem of homelessness affects everyone in the community. Homelessness is such a politically hot potato that it is becoming another one of those taboo party conversations that you steer away from—just like politics and religion.

Decades and decades have passed without the resolve to end such an epidemic. The federal government alone spends one billion dollars each year to help the homeless. One billion! That doesn't include all of the private, corporate, and foundation contributions to the cause. And yet, homelessness doesn't end. Year after year, shelters provide refuge, churches and temples supply meals, downtown missions offer care, social service agencies provide employment training and transitional housing, and developers build affordable housing. Every Thanksgiving season, plastered on the pages of the local newspaper, you see a picture of a tattered homeless child or a hungry toothless homeless man smiling in front of a hot, piping meal, with a headline, "Please Feed the Homeless This Thanksgiving!" The never-ending campaign to raise money for homelessness goes on and on. Yet the problem doesn't end.

It's not as if people are not trying. There are thousands and thousands of Good Samaritans desperately working hard to care for the homeless. But sometimes it feels as if we are simply plugging the holes in the dike rather than preventing the raging waters from overtaking the community. And to make matters worse, some in the community accuse the caregivers of being "poverty pimps," living off of the money donated for the poor. That's like telling the man who is frantically piling sandbags to prevent the flood from overflowing that he is the cause of the flood. It's absurd.

What's wrong with this picture? A rich and powerful country allowing some of its people to live like animals on its streets, scrapping by as if they are in the middle of a famine?

What is wrong with our response?

"It's your fault!"

No, it's your fault!"

The blame game at its worst.

Caregivers trying to stop the flood of human neglect but without the resources or community will to even slow down the raging waters.

This picture obviously needs a touch-up. Or more like a new photo shoot. Something has to be done. It's simply out of control.

Identifying the problem is not the issue. Our communities obviously know we have a significant crisis of homelessness. We see it on freeway off-ramps, at bus stops, in parks and in downtown areas. It's hidden in parked cars, along the bushes of freeways. We see it both in our urban areas as well as in the rural parts of our country. We all know what the problem is.

After years of working on the front lines of homelessness, sitting at the table of community influence-makers, and even writing op-ed pieces for the local paper, I see how absurd this cycle of neglect is in our community. How ridiculous the cycle of blame is. The problem is not going away.

After years of front line service, I've come to one simple conclusion: We don't realize how *absurd* this situation really is in our country. If we could recognize how ridiculous this really is, maybe, just maybe, we might do something about it.

So the goal, here, is not to identify the problem, but instead to recognize the absurdity. Consider this book as an absurd handbook to the homeless situation in our country.

It comes down to one simple perspective. There is only one way for people to see how bizarre and ridiculous we have allowed the state of homelessness to exist and grow in our country. So let us entertain an absurd conclusion:

Maybe, just maybe, we don't really want to end homelessness.

THREE

The Conspiracy

I live in Los Angeles County where experts believe there are 84,000 homeless people on any given night. Granted, even the numerical count of homeless people in America is part of the national debate on homelessness. Some want to say there are only a few thousand homeless people in our country. These are the people who want to deny that there is even a problem. Others, who try to sensationalize the problem—as if it really needs to be embellished more—state there are millions. So somewhere between these two extremes is the truth.

In Los Angeles, there are only 14,000 shelter beds to house homeless people. This number cannot be denied. Subtract the number of shelter beds from the number of homeless people, and the numerical gap is glaring.

If you travel around any city or rural area of our country you will see the significant number of homeless people on the streets. This is a result of not enough temporary shelters and permanent housing for homeless people. In other words, there is a gap between places for homeless people to go and the actual number of homeless people on the streets. That's why we have a problem. In Los Angeles, the gap is large. In our country as a whole, there are hundreds of thousands of homeless people living on our streets.

This is not a new phenomenon. Some of the downtown missions have been serving the homeless for over a hundred years. The spike in the number of homeless increased in the 1980's. This reflects the time when numerous social service agencies were started ten to thirty years ago in response to this growing problem. Clearly, during the last few decades the problem of homelessness has been acute.

So why would the wealthiest and most powerful country in the world allow such statistics on human neglect to exist? And why would we permit it to go on and on for decades? It is absurd that we even have to ask such questions.

I propose an absurd conclusion.

There is a hidden conspiracy in our country. Men and women of power, sitting in smoke-filled, wood paneled boardrooms, high above our urban communities, are scheming and planning this evil conspiracy. They have video screens on the walls, laptop computers on their tables, and internet connections coordinating efforts, pulling electronic levers and pressing the right buttons. An absurd type of "war room" in an effort to control a clandestine effort.

The conspiracy? *To increase homelessness in our community.*

However absurd this may sound, there are clues leaking out of this classified effort, a series of rationales that after looking at the picture again seems nearly logical. These evil-doers have clear reasons why they want to increase homelessness.

Allow me to strip away the camouflage, and let you see for yourself.

Increasing homelessness is good for the economy. It saves our country money. Think of all the funds we would have to spend to house every single homeless person. Think of the cost of training them to obtain a living wage job with benefits. The extraordinary costs to treat their health issues—whether it is substance abuse, mental health, or HIV/AIDS. It is better for our economy to do nothing.

It is good for our self-image. The grueling game of success, keeping up with the Joneses, and the inevitable feeling of not being able to make it, can sometimes have a terrible toll on one's self-image. Add to that the constant barrage of media images of beautiful people that we will never obtain to, beamed through our television sets and movie screens, and clearly we conclude that we need help. Homelessness gives us a temporary reprieve—there's always someone worse off than me.

It makes us feel good. Homelessness gives us a reason to volunteer, to cook those meals on Thanksgiving, so that we can go home and feel good about ourselves afterwards. So we can quench the guilt we might have of over-consumption, of our life of materialism.

It is good for the environment. Who else is going to scavenge the urban landscape of our community to find those discarded soda cans?

Great object lessons for our children. When our kids don't finish their food on their plates, what else would we be able to say? When they stubbornly refuse to do their homework we can threaten them with: "If you don't do your homework you'll end up on the streets!"

A great reason to clean out our closets. After dropping off those plastic bags filled with out-dated clothes, it provides justification to go to Macy's and splurge.

Inexpensive window washing. Much cheaper than that eight dollar drive-through car wash. And it's more convenient than a 7-11 store. Cheap window washing... located at a corner nearest you.

And finally...

What else would you do with all of your spare change? Who needs change anyway, in this dollar-driven economy?

Could there really be a secret society of control-freaks seeking to make our lives better with every pull of the lever and push of the button? The concept is ridiculous. But then again when you look around our country today, the current state of homelessness is just as absurd.

So let's take this logic to the next absurd level. Maybe if we see how ridiculous this situation really is, we will be moved to do something more than just finger-pointing. Maybe we can provide solutions that end homelessness rather than simply manage the problem.

If there is a powerful secret society pushing to increase homelessness, then here is how it to do it...

FOUR

Build Our House On Sand

This is a basic, clear-cut step toward increasing homelessness in your community. Make sure you don't have enough housing units for everyone living in the area. This will dramatically increase the number of homeless people in your neighborhoods and city center.

It is a step based on a principle that I learned in high school economics class - the law of supply and demand: "The supply and demand of goods and services affect prices in a free market economy." For instance, take the price of a loaf of bread that typically would cost about $1.50 each. If the bakers of bread go on strike and stop making it, the supply goes down, and the effect is obvious—not enough bread for everyone. So people are willing to pay a higher price for their loaf of dough, perhaps $2.50 or $3.00. If, on the other hand, there is too much Wonderbread® on the supermarket shelves because no one is buying it (low demand) and they baked too much on that day (high supply), the store will put that bread on the for-sale rack and slice the price in half.

This simple economic formula also has a dramatic affect on the cost of housing. When there are not enough apartments to rent or houses to purchase, the cost goes up. It becomes a scramble, like musical chairs, people pushing and shoving to nab that last available house. And ultimately, in the game of housing, some people lose. Particularly, the homeless.

Is the American Dream of owning your own castle just that—a dream? Those of us who are lucky enough to own a piece of the rock are the fortunate members of the "have" class who can watch our investment asset grow without breaking a sweat. Just this year, alone, the value of a home in Los Angeles County increased 25%. That means if your house was worth $300,000 last year, it is now worth $375,000. Without even lifting a finger, your asset grew $75,000! That's even better than playing the lottery.

No wonder why "have-nots" are tempted to shove dollar bills into the lottery ticket machine in hopes of winning the American Dream. Even if the chance of a winning ticket are so bad, it almost exploits those dreaming of a better life. How can you afford owning your very own home when the price of that home you dream of buying increases more than your annual salary? And it increases that amount every single year.

Is it ludicrous to imagine that the odds of winning the lottery could someday be better than owning a home? I certainly hope not.

Reducing the housing stock also causes another problem: a growing confrontation between builders and activists. That's what's happening in Los Angeles. The builders are renovating old, run down single room hotels or apartments. These places are home to homeless and low-wage earners who can scarcely afford a twelve by twelve foot room with a hot-plate sitting in the closet and a shared bathroom down the hall. The activists abhor the desire of the upwardly mobile urban professionals who dream of loft-living just miles from the workplace.

On the outside it seems simple. Why not rejuvenate decrepit urban centers with high-end residential complexes that hug commercial office towers so people traveling to work don't have to trek hours on the freeway from their suburban hideaways? It's reverse migration, alleviating the decades-old trend of suburban flight. (Was it not the vision of architects, Wright and Le Corbusier, a generation ago, to develop a renaissance of urban centers with towers of work and living spaces, leaving the country-side free of urban, or in today's terminology—suburban, plight?)

But those who fight for the rights of the homeless and poor cry foul. Gentrification is a sin, they say. Many believe that allowing the gentry, or the high class, to move in and displace the poor and working class is an outrage. The displaced can barely cover a month's rent, let alone purchase high-end residential lofts. To build towers of the American Dream that replace towers of poverty, is surely an insult to those who can only dream of a better life, so say the advocates.

Urban renewal is not so simple. Does renovation trump displacement? Or does displacement justify halting urban renaissance?

The lines are drawn in this contentious debate over urban renewal. The debate is dominated by two groups on opposites ends—those who fight tooth and nail for the rights of the displaced and those who possess bold visions to refurbish a broken-down urban core with high-end residential and commercial structures. One group sues the city, the county and anyone else involved in renewal, halting all visions of progress. The other group fights back with their Armani-clad big business lawyers and continues to develop smaller projects that lie beneath the political radar, creating a trickling effect that slowly changes the character of the city.

What is the result of all this legal and political madness? Bold visions of growth become myopic. Nobody wants to rock the boat. Who wants to be accused of kicking out poor, homeless people from their dilapidated, disgustingly dirty and unsafe residences? And yet doing nothing allows slum conditions to exist, harming both those who are unlucky enough to have to live within these conditions and those who live and work in the surrounding community, enduring this physical and emotional blight on a daily basis.

Everybody loses. The homeless, the working poor, the business owner, the homeowner, the visitor. The community.

All because the number of houses is not enough for the number of people.

It's a sad game of musical chairs. Round and round the people go, peering and lurking into closets and kitchens, hoping for an empty home to rent or buy. But when it's time to snag that precious housing unit, there are always people left out of the circle with no place available. The marketplace, or the simple neglect of good community planning, has cruelly taken away more and more chairs out of the game.

This is the obvious first step for those who want to increase homelessness in their community. Stop building housing. Furthermore, if you want to build residential units, make them million dollar lofts that only a fraction of one percent of the population can afford. Get rid of those run-down residential urban hotels and convert them to high-cost urban living units. You will shoot two birds with one stone—reduce the available affordable housing units and build units that only the cream of the society can afford.

Frankly, it would make more sense to encourage, or even mandate, urban developers to build both high-cost *and* low-cost housing as a way of alleviating the housing crisis for all. (But don't tell those who want to increase homelessness...)

FIVE

Keep Minimum Wage To A Minimum

This works quite well. It's another simple social formula. Pay people as little as possible so that they cannot afford to rent an apartment. A perfect technique to increase homelessness.

Here's how it works. The federal minimum wage is $5.15 per hour. Some states actually offer a higher minimum wage standard than the feds. California, for instance, has a $6.75 per hour minimum. That means if you are working as a security guard, maid, or flipping hamburgers at the lowest pay-scale in Los Angeles you are earning $1,168 per month. Take away your taxes (federal, state, and local income tax, FICA, SDI, etc.) and the bacon you will take home is about $934 each month.

Now it's time to go shopping for an apartment with your grandiose take-home pay. The old musical chair game where—you guessed it—the people on the lowest pay scale lose out. The US Department of Housing and Urban Development estimates that the fair market rent for a one-bedroom apartment in Los Angeles is $674. (If you can actually find an available unit.) Then guess what… you now have only $260 left for the whole month to pay for food, utilities, telephone, transportation, clothing, and incidentals.

It just doesn't add up. You barely have enough money simply for basic food staples.

Just imagine this scenario: You're sitting on the floor in a one-bedroom apartment, probably in a rough neighborhood far from the city center, with no electricity, lights, running water, or telephone. You have no money to get to work to pay for this newly acquired abode, and you're probably wearing second-hand clothes bought from the Goodwill store down the street. But you do have some food to eat—a sack of potatoes, dry milk, bread, cheese, and if you're lucky meat and some vegetables. It sounds like a Dicken's novel. It is a visual image of minimum wage living, a stark example of how people end up homeless.

Now I understand why three families will cram their children into a two-bedroom apartment, or rent an illegally-built squatter unit in a backyard garage. It's the game of survival when the logic of mathematics no longer works. Two plus two used to equal four. Now it equals three or even two. At one time, you could put in a solid forty hours per week of work, and still afford simple living. Now, it's not enough to survive. Forty hard hours of work today means you're still fighting to find that one bedroom apartment to cram your three kids and wife into. And we don't understand why people would rather opt for government assistance than actually find a real job?

Years ago, I traveled to Rio de Janeiro, Brazil and was shocked how their favellas, squatter communities, abutted high-rise luxury hotels. It reminds me today of Los Angeles. Million dollar lofts adjacent to skid row neighborhoods. Are American urban cores becoming the new Third World life? Where the poor struggle for life among the rich. Where a full day's wage at low-end work still keeps a person miles and miles from the American Dream because that wage gets you barely anything?

The social debate over minimum wages is just as contentious as the argument over urban development.

If you raise the living wage then businesses will simply eliminate jobs in order to save money. Some say that for every 10% increase in the minimum wage, 100,000 jobs are eliminated. So what would you rather have? A dead-end job with low wages or no employment at all? Which is the lesser of two evils? It's a powerful argument. I'm not an economist so I can't calculate which is better. But I do know that neither option is acceptable. If we permit low wages that only allow a person a sub-standard life style or if we raise wages too high forcing businesses to cut jobs, then everyone loses.

Who is to say that even if we lowered the minimum wage—God forbid—that jobs would still exist. The job competition today is no longer just between neighbor and neighbor, or graduate and graduate. Today's employment era is now also a global contest.

If you're a telemarketing operator sporting headphones while sitting in a suburban industrial office park in San Bernardino, California, your job could still be threatened by a similar telemarketing operator sitting in a low-rise office suite in New Delhi, India. The outsourcing of employment opportunities to nations outside of America is occurring every day. Software engineers, factory workers, electronics specialists and others are all threatened by the other six billion human beings on this planet. It's a scary thought.

To keep our economic engine purring at a breakneck speed down the road of our free market, we need both a healthy supply of jobs in our community and a healthy standard of wage that allows workers to live sensibly. Is there a solution to delicately balance the two?

Perhaps it would be good to eliminate thousands of jobs that only pay sub-standard wages by raising the minimum wage? What is the happy medium between eliminating low-wage jobs and raising the wage high enough for a person to be able to survive?

Some people advocate for a "living wage" standard that is high enough for a worker to afford housing and life's necessities (rent, utilities, food, telephone, transportation, childcare, healthcare, savings, and incidentals.) Depending on the cost of living in a community, a living wage standard could be 50% to 100% more than minimum wage.

No wonder why businesses freak out when this wage is mentioned. To increase the cost of labor to that level could very well put businesses out of business, they argue. Does this simply eliminate a free market and, instead, become a falsely-inflated market? I'm sure the business community lambasts, "You give them an inch (minimum wage), and they'll take a mile (living wage)."

Somewhere between an inch and a mile, between minimum wage and livable wage, there must be a happy medium.

Wages affect everyone. Whether you are on the high end of the social scale of free market enterprise or the low end at minimum wage, you are affected. Some say that in order for a person or family to survive in this competitive world of a free market economy you must have at least three months of your salary socked away in the bank for a rainy day. If you're making three thousand a month, you need nine thousand in the bank. But how many of us, really, have only a paycheck in the bank, if that?

You don't have to be struggling at the bottom rung of the economic ladder to grasp empty-handed at the idea of three months salary in the bank. I see the sad result in the homeless programs I direct. Former stock brokers, teachers, construction workers, engineers huddle in our homeless programs because they all fell victim to the "one paycheck away" syndrome. With not enough money socked away, one freak accident or stupid personal decision socks them in the face of reality and they end up homeless.

Sadly, many of us, whether poor or rich, are simply a paycheck away. With our lives mortgaged to the brink of personal bankruptcy, some are very likely a few thousand dollars away from homelessness.

Now imagine how the odds are truly stacked against you if you're only making minimum wage. Can you really save a few thousand dollars in the bank when you are only taking home less than a thousand? I may not be a mathematician, but I do know that the math just doesn't add up. At minimum wage, the odds are low that you will find a safe, secure, and decent place to live. And the odds are high that you could very well end up homeless.

So for that secret society of conspirators who dream of ways to increase homelessness in our communities, keeping wages to a bare minimum is an easy way to influence their outcomes.

Ironically, the old adage, "A penny saved, is a penny earned," is truly appropriate for many people today who are barely surviving just above poverty. Because pennies are all they'll be able to save.

SIX

No Free Lunch—Or Bed

The word "homeless shelter" conjures up terrible images of cold, dark warehouses filled with government-issued metal bunk beds. Hundreds of men swarm into a facility, wrapped in thick jackets caked with years of dirt, acting deranged from either drug addiction or mental illness. For many on the outside looking in, the scenario is a blight to the community. These images remind me of some type of Hollywood zombie movie.

"If we want to increase homelessness on our streets, just shut down these homeless shelters. They don't seem to work anyway!" say the critics.

This is not a politically correct attitude, I know. Especially near Thanksgiving and the end-of-the-year holidays. But I sometimes wonder if the thought of eliminating homeless shelters float across people's minds, maybe even while they are dropping coins into Santa's red holiday pot outside of Von's® Supermarket.

Sure, people feel guilty, and perhaps even compassionate, when they read that appeal to help homeless mothers and their children living on the streets. Wouldn't anyone? But, come on. There seems to be a homeless shelter in practically every community now. What is this anyway? A warped government's version of a Hilton® Hotel chain for the homeless? If I have to pay $100 or more for a simple hotel room, why should a person who is homeless get a free bed on my tax-laden dime?

The situation is more complicated than first meets the eye.

The trend today, in most urban and suburban communities, is to clean up the streets. Every morning in San Francisco, before the bustle of business begins its routine, large steam-cleaning trucks roll down the streets sanitizing the sidewalks and roads of this international tourist attraction. It seems to be a good idea. Cleaning up the streets should benefit everyone.

But no, say the advocates of people who are homeless. These machines of cleanliness are actually mechanical wolves in sheep's skins. They are devouring up the only possessions a homeless person has, washing away beds and blankets off the streets. They're "mean streets," these well-intended people shout in defense of the indigent who have no political voice. They have nowhere else to go, no place to store their possessions. Is it fair for a city to unleash its mechanical wolves on these poor homeless sheep?

The debate over homelessness just never ends. Urban redevelopment, minimum wages, and now this... clean streets. Can't we agree on anything? I'm beginning to think that one part of our community is from Mars, while the other part is from Venus.

So instead of shutting down all homeless shelters, perhaps we do the opposite by simply replicating what New York City did. They passed a landmark consent decree that gives a homeless person a right to a shelter bed. That means building enough beds for people who are homeless in your city so that they don't have to sleep on cold, dirty, and unsafe city streets. That makes sense too. Although critics will say that poor, lazy people are just taking advantage of the system, trying to simply get a free bed.

Who deserves a free bed, anyway? If you're able to work, why should you get free room and board? The only people I know who are privileged enough to receive such benefits are college students with parents wealthy enough to pay for dorm life. Should we, the taxpayers, pony up the dollars to house and feed people living on the streets?

Consider the alternative. What if the answer is no. Taxpayers should not have to pay for people's plight— whether self-imposed or imposed by others. What would happen to our first world communities then?

It is actually not hard to imagine. There are many countries around the world that simply cannot afford to care for their poor, whether they philosophically agree or not. So the poor and homeless wash their clothes in the cities' rivers, live in tin shacks on hillsides by confiscating land that they don't own, and resort to survival work and begging.

Years ago, in the middle of my university studies, I traveled throughout several African countries. I visited a couple of major cities on that continent and was simply overwhelmed with the sights and sounds of poverty. Scattered trash, foreign smells, abundance of dirt, destitute living conditions, lack of basic necessities were everywhere. What was most astounding were the terrible images of men with cut-off limbs begging on the streets. One man, half-clothed with dirt on his skin, had only a stump for an arm. Another, with makeshift crutches, had only one foot. They were both on the street corner begging for handouts. They looked at our small group of Americans, with our sympathetic eyes, probably thinking that we would be easy targets for begging. Our guide, obviously wanting to show the best of his country, turned the van quickly. He then yelled out to us in his broken English, "The poor in our country are desperate to get money, any way they can. Some even cut off arms, in hopes people will feel sorry for them." The guide was justifying the lack of response to the poor. Guilt would certainly not be felt by this guide. If the poor were cutting off limbs merely so they didn't have to work and could live off of handouts from others, why should I feel guilty for them? Why should I give?

But when that van drove down the street, escaping the sights of poverty, I still felt guilty. I felt sad. I even felt angry. I was twenty-one years old at the time, and I wanted to change the world. I didn't like a world where people had to cut off their arms and legs in order to receive gifts from others. It just wasn't right. It was shameful. Why did people have to go through such drastic, humiliating, disgusting acts? It just didn't make sense. Those images of limbless men perched on that dirty, noisy Third World urban street corner still linger in my mind today.

If this is the result of a philosophical debate over whether the poor and homeless should be housed, then I say let's house them. Even if a handful do take advantage of the system, it's not fair for those who desperately need help.

So let's combine both responses. New York passes a law that every homeless person has a right to a shelter bed. San Francisco steam cleans its streets in hopes of making their community better. Los Angeles struggles between both solutions, teetering on inaction.

Suppose our communities provided a bed for every un-housed person on the street? Then we give the community the right to dispatch street-cleaning machines to do their job, and the right to enforce ordinances that prevent public urination, begging, loitering, and sleeping in public. Clean streets, but not mean streets.

Wouldn't both parties of each extreme, both Mars and Venus, be placated? Our neighborhoods are clean and secure, and those in need of help are housed, fed, and safe. Sure, there are still many barriers. What happens when more people become homeless? Who is going to pay for all those beds? Are they just going to stay in a shelter all their lives and not transition into self-sufficiency? In what neighborhoods are you going to build these shelters? Don't these people really need permanent housing, not temporary housing?

Questions. Always questions in a debate. If there were easy answers, we probably wouldn't have a homeless problem in our communities.

I once sat down with the mayor of a fairly small city in Southern California that struggles with a significant problem of homelessness. A few years before, there was an official count of homeless people in that city. I proposed to him that the city fund enough beds for each homeless person in the city, which would have been a total of $5.8 million each year. Just about the same amount of money that was already in the city's budget for homeless services. Then pass citywide public nuisance ordinances that would basically clean up the streets.

Although the solution seems over-simplified, the same questions arose. Who, where, what? Questions that seem to halt any progression.

Questions without simple answers should not immobilize a community. Doing nothing means that everyone in the community loses.

Why don't we start by housing everyone living on the streets? Then deal with the long-term solutions of permanent housing, mental health care, substance abuse treatment, and employment training. Wouldn't that be a more compassionate first step to simply doing nothing? It makes sense to me.

Then again, if you want to increase homelessness simply close down all the existing homeless shelters. That would certainly work.

SEVEN

The Homeless Outlaw

Let's just arrest homeless people and throw them in jail. That'll get them off the streets.

Some people actually embrace this way of thinking. They would rather pass laws that outlaw homelessness without providing the funding and political will to offer alternative housing and services. Ironically, people think outlawing homelessness is a valid solution, when it's actually an excellent way to increase the problem instead.

Unless a person living on the street commits a violent felony, if arrested for a non-violent offense, he will end up back on the street within days. This useless cycle of arrest and release, arrest and release, does nothing to help that person other than keeping him from actually dealing with personal issues that could help him transition into permanent housing.

In fact, outlawing homelessness is essentially the same as setting up a government-run homeless shelter system. Think about it. Throw everyone on the streets in jail, and the jail becomes a homeless shelter with locked doors, armed guards, and barbed wire fences. Except the jail bed costs twice as much as a privately-run shelter bed with supportive services. Jail becomes an expensive babysitting service, while a homeless program provides transitional services to help a person get off the streets.

Of course, proponents of outlawing homelessness would never label homeless people as "outlaws." That's just not politically correct. But many in our community would still urge stronger ordinances—but not "laws", they say, as if there's a difference—banning public urination, sleeping on the streets, aggressive pan handling, and public drunkenness. It certainly makes sense in a perfect world.

Critics, however, would say these public nuisance ordinances are actually cloaked as ways to criminalize homeless people. Is it fair for a person who has no place to sleep to be arrested for snoozing on a park bench? Is it right for a person who has to relieve himself in the alley be cited when there are no public toilets available?

I sometimes imagine myself in the same predicament. If I was homeless, and every shelter bed in town was filled, where would I go to sleep? Where could I go without worrying about someone trying to hurt me or having the police harass me? On the beach? In the bushes in a quiet park, under a freeway bridge in Hollywood? I don't think I would ever get a good night's sleep, worrying that every faint noise I hear could be someone trying to harm me. I just can't imagine such a predicament. Sadly, the nightmare scenario would be worse for a female huddled with her children on the streets.

Yet, both sides of the argument continue to tug their strong wills in their opinionated direction, as if it's a tug-of-war with three hundred pound linebackers on each end of the rope stubbornly sitting on the ground not willing to budge. It becomes a standstill with no one willing to propose a compromise solution. A little tug here, and a little tug there. The debate goes one way and then the other. But no one seems to win.

Solutions to homelessness in our country end up at a standstill. So the approaches to the problem continue.

Some public officials are dusting off an old 1970's New Jersey community program that sought to improve the quality of community life by increasing police activity on a basic, front lines level. To encourage law enforcement to walk the streets in order to project a safer and more secure neighborhood. It was called the "Safe and Clean Neighborhoods Program."

In the 1980's a re-invention of this program transformed it from more than just projecting a safer neighborhood into a fear-reducing, neighborhood clean-up program called, "Broken Windows." The approach was simple. Many people feared violent crime, but were also afraid of being bothered by disorderly people—you know, the drunks, mentally ill, vagrants. Basically, the homeless. In order to reduce major crimes, law enforcement must reduce minor crimes and community blight. That means ordinances against public nuisance activities, and activities to clean up blight—graffiti, illegal dumping, and broken windows.

It's the old "there goes the neighborhood" perspective. You know, when the neighbor down the street stops mowing his lawn and leaves beat-up old cars in his driveway, and the place starts looking like a run-down shack from the other side of the railroad track. The rest of the neighbors freak out thinking that the whole area is going down hill.

This is the justification for approving public nuisance ordinances. You deal with the bad seed of a neighbor down the street and the community returns to its pristine-looking Ozzie and Harriet neighborhood we all still dream about.

Deal with the homeless problem through stronger police action, and we're back to the future—the 1950's become today. A mom and a dad with 2.5 children living behind a white picket fenced post-World War Two suburban home. But certainly no homeless people sporting tattered cardboard signs at street corners. If only it was as simple as Michael J. Fox driving a souped-up Delorean back to the future. And our dreams would come true.

Unfortunately, the 2000's are not the 1950's. And unfortunately, law enforcement on their own, cannot solve this terrible community dilemma of people sleeping on the streets. Undoubtedly, law enforcement must be one important piece of the solution pie, they just can't be the whole pie.

Consider two other important parts to this difficult puzzle.

First, ensure there are enough homeless services and housing, including emergency and transitional beds along with affordable permanent housing units, before implementing ordinances that ban public nuisance activities. Without such practical alternatives, issuing citations for quality of life offenses simply feeds the cycle of arrest and release, arrest and release, without truly dealing with appropriate solutions. Think about it. Is a homeless person really going to dramatically transform his ways on the street simply because he was issued a citation? It's more like he will ignore the citation and allow it to turn into an arrest warrant. Then the courts get bogged down with non-essential cases, and jails get clogged up with people who just need a bed.

So the second part to this social puzzle is just as essential. Here in Los Angeles, a group of social service providers (PATH, Midnight Mission, Public Counsel, Union Rescue Mission, Volunteer Center of Los Angeles, and Volunteers of America), along with city and county law enforcement agencies, court and legal system, and political officials have joined together. They offer an alternative-sentencing program that is creative and encourages participation in social services rather than arrests. We call it SOS, Streets or Services.

When a person on the street violates a quality-of-life ordinance, he is given the option to participate in a social service program rather than being arrested and booked. It gives a person direct access to services that could very well help him overcome his homelessness. It reduces the caseload of the court and law enforcement system, and helps the overall community by transitioning people living on the streets into housing and service programs.

Another movement sweeping the country is the Homeless Court. This is an alternative-sentencing program for homeless people who allow their non-violent, quality-of-life citations to turn into arrest warrants. Rather than being arrested they are given a sentence that typically mandates participation in a social service program—it could mandate substance abuse treatment, employment training, or even getting a high school diploma.

Transforming big stick law enforcement consequences into practical, compassionate, and life-changing programs provides powerful solutions to our community homeless crisis. Let the extremists entrench their arguments into polarizing positions. Just arrest the homeless and throw the key away. Or, eliminate all public nuisance laws, and let people do whatever they want on the streets as long as they don't hurt someone else. These stubborn positions can be shouted throughout community meetings, op-ed pages, and television commentaries until their voices get hoarse. But we all know that these positions provide no solutions.

To outlaw homelessness simply encourages the increase of homelessness. So for those conspirators wanting to bolster the numbers of homeless in our communities, simply bring out the big guns of law enforcement:

"Watch out, there's a new sheriff in town. And he means business!"

EIGHT

Don't Ask, Don't Plan

Could you imagine architect Frank Gehry building L.A.'s Disney Hall without a plan? The design might have been even crazier than the current one, and who knows if the structure would've withstood a California earthquake. Thankfully, to most Angelino's, Gehry developed a beautifully articulate plan for a structure that has become a Los Angeles landmark.

A good plan is important for designers of buildings, architects of war, teachers, writers, engineers, anyone planning for the future.

So here is the best-kept secret on how to increase homelessness. Ready? When people are discharged from jail, mental health facilities, foster care, or health care, whatever you do, don't ask them if they have a place to go. That way if they possess no plan they end up homeless. Bingo. More homeless people on the streets.

It is amazing how simple cause and effect can be.

If a visitor from out of town visits my home, the first conversation is about where they are staying. A polite gesture to make sure they have a place to go.

You would think a similar gesture would be provided for people leaving government institutions. Instead, every day people are being released without anywhere to go.

Looming near downtown Los Angeles are two large windowless structures that locals call the "twin towers," but it's not a *Lord of the Rings* movie set. Rather than urban professionals crouching over laptops and fax machines, what's housed in these urban edifices are people arrested for simple nonviolent offenses along with offenders who commit major crimes. It is Los Angeles County's main jail that houses convicted jaywalkers who allow their citations to turn into warrants, along with violent murderers who prey on others.

Then quietly, amidst the bustle of the city's operations, while office workers are commuting to and from work and venders are selling their wares, the jail releases 350 to 500 people each day onto the streets. Most have no place to go.

It has become a pipeline of low-income and homeless humanity gushing onto the sidewalks, gutters, and alleys of our central city. Sadly, to some people, they are considered human waste who waste away their own lives along with our community resources. So they are pigeon-holed into neighborhoods where nobody wants them. We call it Skid Row.

Skid Row. A derogatory term created years ago when the down-and-out "bums" in the Northwestern logging industry would hang out where the logs skidded down the mountains to the waterways below. Now we see it as a place where human life has skidded to the bottom rung of the social ladder, where people have given up on their personal hopes and dreams, where futures scream to a halt.

Small little cardboard pup tents propped up against urban concrete block buildings. Rows and rows of them, lined up on urban sidewalks, as if they are meant to be there. We drive by them ignoring their predicament, pretending that human beings do not sleep in these temporary street structures. Pretending that this is just an apocalyptic horror movie that we can walk out of after sitting through a couple of hours of terror. But no matter how much we want to wish them away, they're still there. People skidding down life's path onto our public streets.

Our streets become their bedroom, living room, and unfortunately, their bathroom.

It's no wonder that businesses and homeowners living near this predicament are screaming for help. Imagine if dozens and dozens of Greyhound buses filled with homeless people dropped off their passengers in your neighborhood. Imagine if they started erecting cardboard pup tents on your streets, near the stores you shop at, along the route where your children walk to school. There would be a town hall meeting faster than you could snap those electric locks on a Cadillac.

Everyone loses when nothing happens. Certainly people without homes would rather sleep in an apartment than in a cardboard pup tent. Certainly homeowners and businesses would rather see these people thriving in employment and permanent housing than being arrested or living in squalor.

Everyone knows there's a problem, and we all want to solve it. We just can't agree on what direction.

So our community continues to allow the "don't ask, don't plan" policy of discharge planning. Like the military's procedure of "don't ask, don't tell" approach to gays in the armed forces, many think it's better to turn our heads and pretend it will just go away.

But those darn cardboard pup tents keep popping up in our urban cores. Wishing away the problem just won't work. You can close your eyes and wish as hard as you can, but there will still be homeless people tucked away in a propped up lean-to until something changes. The flow of discharged humans from public institutions will continue until someone, hopefully the right ones, will just ask a simple question... Do you have a place to go?

Why don't they just ask? You don't have to be a rocket scientist to figure this out. Why doesn't a social worker or discharge worker ask the former inmate, patient, or client if they have a place to go?

Perhaps they fear the wrong answer. What if the person says, "I have nowhere to go."? Then what? A pat on his back and a quick, "Oh well. Good luck. Don't let the door hit you on the backside on your way out!" That basically means a free ticket to Skid Row.

If you don't ask where he plans to go and you don't plan for his housing future, then you don't have to pay for his next step in life. Otherwise, it is going to cost money. Back to the old "no one deserves a free bed" mentality.

Think of the cost for the jail system, hospital, mental health institution, if they had to cover the cost of housing everyone discharged from their care. It's much easier on their pocketbook to simply open the exit door and wish their discharged person well: "Good luck, and don't let the Skid Row bedbugs bite."

So who pays to stop the flow of discharged humanity from gushing into our communities? The institution that releases them? The local government that receives them? The homeless service provider that is supported through private donors like you? Uncle Sam? Someone has to pay. Otherwise, we all pay for this community neglect. We all pay when we simply don't ask, and don't plan.

Wouldn't it be easier to cut the flow before it starts? Perhaps we could place social workers and housing specialists in these institutions to help people plan for their housing future before they are discharged? They could sign up for government funded housing vouchers, work with employment training programs, connect with transitional housing providers, reconnect with estranged family members. All before they are released from their program.

It must certainly be easier to work with people who are already in a program than starting from scratch with people flushed out of the system. People who are now accustomed to Skid Row squalor life.

It is certainly obvious that our communities need to develop a comprehensive discharge planning process for everyone leaving public institutions. It just makes sense. A community-wide plan is just as practical as an individual housing plan for every discharged person in the system.

Please. No more dumping busloads of people into our neighborhoods and urban cores. This is certainly one solution on which everyone would agree!

NINE

The Leaf Blower Mentality

You hear the stories. The police chief of a small Midwestern town gives the local town drunk a one way bus ticket to Los Angeles, or San Francisco, or New York. Anywhere, as long as he doesn't return.

I hear these adages over and over again. States sending homeless people into other states. One-way bus tickets are issued, or personal escorts transport people across the state line. Coincidentally, it has also become a local activity. Even within communities throughout Los Angeles they point the finger at each other. Are Beverly Hills police dropping homeless off in Santa Monica, Long Beach dropping them off in Inglewood, Los Angeles to West Hollywood? Many cities are blaming other cities for their homeless problem.

What is going on? Is it a secret underground shuttle system of homeless people? Where communities frustrated or simply exhausted of this human blight join this hush-hush national scheme of human transfers, blowing away these human community stains off our neighborhood palates?

Communities are resorting to a leaf blower mentality. They put their masks on to cover the taste and smells of homelessness, pack their mechanical blowers on their backs, crank up the engines of change, and blow these people away, into other communities, into other states. Like people are homeless leaves fallen from trees, scattered on the streets, annoying the community.

Ironically, this leaf blower approach to solving homelessness simply increases the problem. So what if you drop a homeless person off in another city, or give them a one-way ticket out of town. Without dealing with the causes of that person's homelessness, the problem will continue to fester.

Could this be part of the conspiracy to increase homelessness?

To move people who are homeless from one community to another is like a couple of four year olds shoving chess pieces across the board without any concept of the game. Things get knocked down, pieces get shifted around with no sense of direction, and nobody wins.

More and more communities are throwing their hands up in disgust and frustration with homelessness. They just don't know what to do. Then the business community and homeowner associations start putting the pressure on the cities. We're losing business! Our school children are not safe! Tourists are staying away! So if you're a politician or city official with your most fervent voter groups and core taxpayer base clamoring for change, what do you do?

Most communities are tempted to send out the forces. It's the big-stick mentality once again. Deploy your police officers to sweep the homeless out of your neighborhoods. Of course, this response is not going to be as obvious as dispatching forces clad with riot gear and batons. Again, not a politically correct response. Instead, bring a couple of social workers to tag along with the sweeping police force, and now it becomes more palatable.

It is a short-term answer for those hollering for a solution.

I was told that at one time, there was a beachfront town in Southern California that posted on their city website where groups could help "feed the homeless." Coincidentally, the locations were at *another* beachfront town miles away from its own community. In other words, if your group is going to attract homeless people through your compassionate feeding program, please attract them in another community, not ours. Was this intentional? It definitely fits the leaf blower mentality. Let another community solve the problem. It's easier, less costly, and efficient.

Unfortunately, for communities who instill this leaf blower approach to homelessness, people who have no homes are mobile. Sure, for some of the most visible homeless people in our communities, the ones that are always at the same street corner or bus bench, they almost seem anchored to their spots. But for a majority of people they move from community to community, looking for food, shelter, and services. Keeping one step beyond the arm of the law or moving from others who might harm them. Others are mobile because they are forced out of the pipelines of public institutions or placed on this underground human shuttle system from community to community.

However, if you sweep them out of one community and into another, it is a sure bet they will return. There is a lack of shelter, housing, and services throughout our country. So if a person is forced into another community that is deficient of services, what makes you think they will stay? If they have already found a safe hiding place under a bridge, in the bushes along the freeway, or in a park, they will return to their haven.

If the receiving community gets fed up with their homeless problem they will just instill the same leaf blower approach as all the others. So now the response to homelessness among communities becomes a shoving match. The bulked-up arms of the law start pushing what some extremists might think are human waste out of one neighborhood and into another, only to have others do the same.

A quiet match of shoving and pushing, pushing and shoving commences. People sleeping on the streets become human pinballs in our society's pinball machinery. They are bounced around one neighborhood to another, except most people do not hear the whistles and bells of this sad societal game. The sweeps usually occur late at night or early in the morning when most housed people are cocooned in their own bedrooms. Nobody really wants to watch this game.

Humans bouncing around our neighborhoods as if they're beachballs tossed among the crowd at a sports stadium. But there's no whooping and hollering, unless it's the displaced homeless people themselves. Police departments tire of this back and forth, cat and mouse contest of wills. Certainly many would say they could be doing more than just fixing "broken windows".

So another form of police enforcement pops up. Businesses band together to hire private security companies to do the police's bidding. They put on green or purple-colored polo shirts and patrol neighborhoods.

Is it another form of vigilante? A private police force imposing the "broken window" theory on a community in fear of lawlessness and blight? Or is it a practical alternative to assisting a community's already under-funded, overworked police force? Certainly, businesses should have the right to safeguard their own community shouldn't they?

On the streets of Hollywood Boulevard, the shirts of a private security company, Burke Security, are seen everywhere. They were hired by the Hollywood Entertainment District, a local business improvement district that wanted to develop a creative, more compassionate response to homelessness in their business community. These security officers are patrolling a tourist attraction that could very well go under if the streets do not stay clean, free of trash and free of the sights of homelessness and poverty. This community response is different, however. Many of the private patrol officers also act as peer social workers for people in need. I've seen them encouraging runaway youth and homeless adults to enter social services. They become street outreach workers seeking to help people transition off the streets.

Could vigilante justice transform into street social work? If so, then everyone wins. Mars no longer fights with Venus. Certainly, this could become a practical goal for those tempted to simply sweep away the homeless.

I once received a telephone call from a nationally-known celebrity who suggested that we simply bus all of the homeless people currently living in the cities to a social service camp out in the desert where they can receive training and services. Although his suggestions were proposed with good intentions, his solution to a very complicated societal problem was a common reaction from a community tired of this relentless community blight. Pick them up and ship them somewhere else.

It is almost a form of internment like one group of Americans had to endure during World War Two. Round up these people that are a threat to national or community security and ship them off to an internment camp in the desert.

This is a reactive solution that didn't work fifty years ago, and certainly would not work today.

That leaf blower approach to solving homelessness, however, is so tempting. It is an enticement that lingers before us because it is an immediate—albeit shortsighted—solution. Ship them out, and the problem is solved, at least in our community. We like instant, quick-acting problem solvers. But as the old saying goes—if it sounds too good to be true, it probably is too good to be true.

Homeless people in our community become like the dust in the wind, irritants to our eyes and spread around everywhere. It is hard to see clearly beyond the limited shortsighted solutions that we grasp in desperation. Many communities don't see that the leaf blower mentality is a desperate myopic solution that does nothing to solve homelessness.

TEN

Access Denied

What do you do when you don't want your small child to grab the pots and pans on the stove, or get medicine in the cupboard, or nab those fresh-baked cookies on the kitchen counter? You move things just beyond the reach of their tiny grasping hands and limit their access.

Do the same thing by limiting access to services that people living on the streets need, and you will increase homelessness.

Why would any community do such a thing, you might ask? Why would a community limit access to social services for people in need? It just doesn't make sense. Can you picture homeless people standing on their toes reaching as far as they can above their heads in hopes of grasping the hand of a social worker standing above them with no avail? It's a sickening picture of a system that has gone bad. Could it be true?

Look around, however, and you see glimpses of a broken system everywhere.

Grab a map of your community and place push-pins where the community services are located. The free health clinic is here and the homeless shelter is there, the mental health program is in that neighborhood and the employment training program is over there. They are spread out all over the landscape, tossed about like a bunch of jacks on the floor with no connection other than bus lines.

So when a person who is homeless is in need of a doctor's visit and a place to find a job, he has to take a ride on a bus route to one place, wait for an appointment, and then jump on another bus across town to access the other service. He would never make it.

I once asked a person in our program how long it took for her to go from service to service. She said at least a full day if she went to two agencies. More than two, and she would have to spend another day riding the bus.

This kind of community social service system is great if efficiency, timeliness, and access are not important.

In most communities throughout our country people in poverty or without homes are carted around town on public transportation, crisscrossing neighborhoods in search of services. Their stonewalled faces peer out of bus windows, hurting from lack of food, healthcare, or housing, as they pass by homes filled with people who simply don't relate to their predicament.

When you think about this system of care-giving, it is almost an evil tease. Like parents controlling their children's cable television access so their kids are only allowed to watch boring news talk shows while the parents enjoy cartoons in the other room.

We place services all over the community so that access for people on the lowest rung of the economic ladder is limited. Then we make them walk or travel on public transportation as they trek through neighborhoods in which they could only dream of living. We dangle much needed services in front of them, but then spread the services all over the community so they're difficult to access.

A director of a human service department in a California city once told me that he tried to experience this shuttle-bus system of providing services. So he jumped on a bus to travel throughout his city to see how long it took to access different service agencies. He said it was not only time consuming, it was confusing. If it's confusing for a well-paid, social service expert, imagine what it means for a scraping-the-bottom-of-the-barrel low-income person desperately hurting for services.

Thankfully, there is actually a perfectly good solution to this system of madness.

What is the trend for most customer-based institutions during this time of cutthroat business competition? It is providing better access to potential customers by building Super-Store centers, ala Wal-Mart and Best Buy, or construct megamalls where buyers can flock in droves with access to every consumer good they can dream of purchasing. We are becoming a country of malls and superstores. It is a system of easy access for our consumer-driven economy. We can park our car in the large lots surrounding these structures of consumerism, and have access to shopping, a haircut, a ride on a merry-go-round, a nice restaurant, and see the latest blockbuster flick.

So why don't we do the same for people in need of social services? Ask all the service agencies in the community to locate their services in one place, so people without homes need only to travel to one location rather than all over the city. It becomes a system of co-location where agency services share the overhead cost of one facility, coordinate their services with each other while people in need have easy access.

We provide this solution here in Los Angeles. We call it the PATH Mall where nearly two dozen public and private social service agencies are housed in mall suites in a bright, colorful, open, clean, dignified setting. The un-housed people in Los Angeles have access to dozens and dozens of services all on one site, including employment training, mental health care, substance abuse treatment, health care, legal services, high school education, haircuts and facials, and even an on-site court to deal with outstanding warrants.

Can you imagine having lost your job and consequently your apartment, only to find yourself at the front door of a homeless agency? Images of dirty, alcohol-reeking homeless men flash across your imagination as you practically shake in your boots with fear of entering a world of homelessness.

When you walk into the PATH Mall, however, the colors and brightness almost blind you. It's not dark and dungy, an assumption just before you walked in, instead it's like the mall down the street. Except the store signs now list the agency services—Employment, Housing, Education, Beauty Salon, Community Court.

It's a dream come true for anyone living on the streets. It is a dream for anyone working in social services that is frustrated over the lack of coordination between agencies.

There was once a homeless person standing in the courtyard in front of our main entrance one early morning. He was screaming at the top of his lungs at imaginary intruders, swinging his fists into the air. Even people used to street life were concerned and afraid.

So we sent outside a staff member from the substance abuse agency and another from the mental health clinic to talk with this clearly disturbed person. After calming him down and talking to him, they ruled out severe mental illness and concluded he was high on some illegal drug. The substance abuse counselor was able to intake the individual into his program to diffuse the situation.

A new system of co-location of services works.

Just think if this out-of-control person had walked into a traditional homeless service outlet. Like you're really going to give him a bus token and instruct him to get his own mental health assessment across town, and then have him trek across town to another site for a substance abuse treatment program. The old way of spreading services all over town just doesn't work.

Imagine building these malls of social services strategically placed throughout large cities where homeless people congregate. No longer will they have to take an urban journey on lines of public transportation, teased by the neighborhoods of wealth, frustrated by time delays and disoriented through the web of maps and stations. Clearly, it is a system of denying access to the most vulnerable citizens in our community.

Now it's simply a walk down a mall corridor filled with every service that a homeless person needs. Eye candy for people hurting from sickness, disoriented from mental illness, desperate for employment, or in need of housing. What the *Mall of America* is for middle class America, this becomes for homeless America.

Instead of Bloomingdale's, Sears, and Macy's, the anchor stores of this new kind of mall become employment centers, health clinics, mental health programs, and substance abuse treatment sites. This, along with the usual beauty salon and food service court.

Deny a person access to services and a community increases homelessness. Provide every service that a person needs under one roof and the dream of ending homelessness becomes closer to reality.

ELEVEN

Fostering Homelessness: One Emancipated Youth At A Time

Eighteen is a magic number here in America. At this age, you can join the army, vote for your favorite politician, work any fulltime job you want, and get married without parental consent.

This is also the age when the foster care system immediately discharges you from their system. Never mind that you might still be overwhelmed with side affects of early childhood abuse or still possess the tendency to commit a criminal act, you are eighteen and are no longer supported by the county. Out you go, so we can fill your bed with the next dysfunctional child.

This has become another excellent human pipeline spilling homelessness onto the streets of America. For many youths discharged from the system, they receive a free ticket out of their nightmare childhoods only to walk through a gateway that deposits them directly into a state of homelessness. Over one quarter of all homeless adults living in shelters across the country have endured America's foster care system. So says a national HUD study. Not a good statistic if you're evaluating the success of the foster care system.

Since when does eighteen become a magical age on the road to adulthood anyway? At this age, why does our system choose to immediately release foster youth with backgrounds of physical and sexual abuse, criminal behavior and emotional neglect? As if at this age they instantly become mature, responsible, motivated adults ready to find a job and rent an apartment.

Ask any parent struggling with a rebellious teenager if age eighteen magically turns this child into a mature adult, and you'll get the answer to why the foster system has become a broken rail system to homelessness.

Our country won't allow eighteen year olds to drink or purchase alcohol, and yet will force them to find a job and rent an apartment even if the baggage they carry is more emotional than physical.

Is it the foster care system's responsibility to help that young child or teen empty his emotional baggage before he turns eighteen? Is it perhaps the foster parents' responsibility? Someone has to help these children unpack their emotional luggage in order to give them a chance to live in a stable home life.

Why are we dealing with this growing, almost sadistic, problem that haunts biological and foster families throughout our community? There certainly must be a better safety net for children enduring abusive family lives, families experiencing mutinous teenagers, and youth on the verge of hardcore criminal lifestyles. Our foster care safety net has a large hole in it that allows many of these kids to fall onto our streets.

What can be done? U.S. Senator Hillary Clinton proposes the "it takes a village" solution to raising children.

When there are problems within a family's web of relationships, the whole village must rally around them with support and care.

Nowadays, in our fast-paced progressive lifestyle that village concept has evaporated. Our families barely make it with two-income households, figuring out childcare payments and logistics, praying that employment continues, juggling children's education and extracurricular activities, and just trying to eat dinner together every night. You almost need a physics degree to figure out how to juggle all of these family responsibilities at once.

Throw in a few dysfunctional activities into a family's routine—drug use, physical abuse, mental illness, criminal behavior, neglect—and the system breaks down. Bingo. Another foster care placement into the system. It never fails.

Where is the village in all of this? Your extended family units are all dealing with the same dilemma—keeping those darn balls in the air at the same time. There's not much time to help each other out when you're trying to keep your own family afloat. This is not the Mennonite lifestyle where life is simple and pure. That life left most of America decades and decades ago.

Unfortunately, today the village concept of a safety net is left to government institutions like the foster care system. If a child is in physical danger there is no village system to protect him from his own family other than the government. So the authorities step in, sometimes with armed police, to escort a frightened child into a system of foster care that is just as frightening as the life they left. Government becomes the default village for dysfunctional family life.

Sadly, if that child is still in the system at eighteen years of age, he has a one in four chance that he will end up homeless. Not great odds for a village system run by government officials desperately responding to hurting and abused family situations. Like homelessness, the foster care system is just as inundated with people in need of help.

There are some interesting programs out there that are providing a ray of hope. One unique agency here in Los Angeles is called *Childshare*. They mobilize families of faith groups into taking foster children into their homes. What is so unique about that, you might be wondering? The key to this program, however, is not to simply find another willing family to help alleviate the foster system of care. The emphasis of the program is to network families of faith groups together as a built-in system of support—they become a village.

Raising an adolescent in a family is difficult enough. Add to this mixture a history of sexual abuse or criminal behavior and what family could truly overcome the odds of preparing this child for adulthood? The family needs a village of support to succeed. Hence, a network of families from local faith groups becomes the instant village. What the government program, deficient of funding and staff, lacks is what this village of families can provide— babysitting services, peer support, personal advice, opportunities to mourn, laugh, and cry together. A net that surrounds your family.

This safety net becomes stronger, held together by families all experiencing the same thing. If we tighten this net as snug as possible the holes of the system get smaller. Small enough that they keep children from falling through.

We dream of our children becoming doctors, engineers, lawyers, professionals in our growing and active world. We pray they build healthy families of their own, cocooned in their own homes, safe and secure. We hope their relationships stay positive and healthy, their view of the future filled with hope. Nobody, not anyone, would willingly dream of their children entering a system of care whose outcome results in one in four becoming homeless.

It's just not thinkable.

So while families in our community struggle to be whole, fight the demons of abuse, ward off temptations of drugs, and defend themselves from victimization, the system that takes in the human by-products of such struggles must be fixed. We have to create an environment for these children to grow up into adulthood filled with hope, overwhelmed with a conviction that they can overcome their past's demons and walk on a path of emotional health.

We must help these children enter the gates of adulthood by gaining the tools to find employment, by providing professional support to overcome mental health issues, and helping them to live independently. A tough call given the fact that these children have been tossed from family to family, controlled by judges, social workers, and foster families. But it can be done, especially if a village system of support is developed.

What is our other option? Let them flounder in a spiraling system of neglect until they end up on our streets with no hope or ability to become independent? Our streets are already filled with graduates of our foster care system; the only degree they possess is an ability to survive bad things. That includes homelessness.

Fostering homelessness one emancipated youth at a time could very well be a hidden agenda among conspirators who seek to increase homelessness. It's the trickle-down theory of increasing homelessness. No one will ever know because these kids practically become "nobodies" on the street. Open the spigot of the homeless pipeline one drop at a time and our community will never know what hit them.

From foster care to homelessness. It is an obscenely absurd rite of passage for those living on the streets of America today.

TWELVE

Eliminate Welfare

Here's another infamous story that has affected our perspective of people living in poverty, and specifically people supported by welfare.

Decades ago, a former U.S. President coined the memorable term "welfare queen" when he described a welfare-cheating mother living in Chicago who used 80 false names, 30 different addresses, and several fictitious dead husbands to bilk the welfare system of hundreds of thousands of our tax dollars. Today, those welfare queens driving their welfare Cadillacs through the streets of ghetto America are still lodged into our perception of poverty and homelessness.

The temptation to simply eliminate welfare fraud by disbanding the system altogether is not a surprising response given the sickening images of fraud painted onto the canvas of public opinion. Abolishing the system, however, would also take almost six million people off of government welfare rolls and put many, if not all, on the verge of homelessness.

But is that welfare queen image true? Critics of the former President say she never existed. It was a myth to encourage America to reform, if not eliminate, the welfare system. And like the spotting of live Elvis sightings, the infamous welfare queen seemed to be popping up everywhere. I remember while living in Pasadena, California, some people pointed to a large home overlooking the Rose Bowl and told me that the welfare queen used to live in that house, a garage filled with Cadillacs and a house packed with designer furniture. The myth would just not die.

Clearly, if there were thousands and thousands of these welfare queens sitting pretty on our tax-paying dime then this fraud would have been exposed years ago. I am certain there are a handful of people who take advantage of the system, able to receive public benefits when they could very well be working. But driving Cadillacs and making a hundred thousand dollars a year? Let's get real.

So do we throw the baby out with the bath water? Eliminate a system that prevents nearly six million people from becoming homeless because a handful of recipients should really be working rather than receiving free benefits? Those greedy, selfish takers that abuse the system muddy the waters to the point that everyone should simply be tossed out, the dirty water and the innocent baby. Is this the solution? Some people would say, "Yes!. It's better for the baby to be tossed out than to sit in the dirty water!"

Critics of our current welfare state would say that this was not the vision of former President Lyndon Johnson when he began the "War on Poverty" back in 1964. To fight this war, he pledged to develop a job corps, a community action program, a volunteer program, a whole government department to fight poverty. He told Congress "for the first time in our history, it is possible to conquer poverty."

Forty years later, however, the war continues unabated. The critics would argue that government-funded programs to combat poverty just don't work.

So a decade ago, Congress sought to reform the welfare system. "End Welfare As We Know It" was the mantra of that day. The government cost of entitlement at that time was nearly a quarter of a trillion dollars—that's trillion with a 't'—and projected to go higher. People receiving welfare were not finding jobs, instead were creating a welfare culture where the daughters ended up in the same system as the mothers.

A broken and toothless system of care was reformed. Recipients had to now work or look for work to be eligible for public benefits. And the kicker... You only received public assistance for a maximum of five years. Welfare was no longer a lifelong entitlement. This certainly ended welfare as we know it

Did it work? As the recipients max out of their five-year limit many critics are looking to see if they have found jobs and become self-sufficient. Some experts say yes and others say no. It is the same old Mars and Venus perspective on social problems.

Have we, as a society, become mean-spirited, picking on people who cannot defend or support themselves? Are we not a country that values compassion and humane acts for those less fortunate than us? Again, some would say yes, and others no.

Advocates of public entitlements have started to turn the tables around. If you're going to criticize public entitlements for the poor then please look at the others receiving similar if not more benefits.

Advocates have pointed their sights on corporate America. So rather than looking at welfare queens driving their mythical Cadillacs, how about those corporate CEO's cruising in the back of their company-owned limousines? Their lifestyles of the rich and famous paid for by generous government subsidies. For example, in the late 1980s and early 1990s a government bailout of failed Savings & Loans cost the taxpaying public $500 billion. And when Congress and the President propose large pork-barrel spending bills that emphasize privatization of government programs, tax breaks, or government subsidies to corporations they are basically proposing public welfare dollars to corporate America, so say the welfare advocates.

If we are going to be fair, let's point our arrows at everyone dependent on public support—both the poor and the rich, the welfare queen and the corrupt corporate CEO. No one should be excused for getting rich on tax dollars that are meant to help the needy. The culture of welfare can doom both the impoverished family able only to see beyond their food stamps and monthly check as well as the government-dependent business able only to make a profit with the help of Uncle Sam.

Are we creating class warfare between the poor and the rich when both ends of the socio-economic ladder are fighting for their rights for government entitlements? The desperate hands of the poor are raised up trying to grasp that monthly welfare check while the privileged hand of the rich swoop down to grab their own entitlements. It is an absurd system gone amuck.

If we're going to eliminate welfare as we know it, let's eliminate entitlements for both the poor and the rich. If we're going to throw out the baby with the bath water, let's also throw out the fat cat with his bottles of Perrier water.

Entitlements cut both ways. If we cut one group's welfare, then we eliminate the other's subsidies. Plain and simple. If this actually occurred—equitable elimination on both ends of government entitlements—then surely reasonable minds would come together. One group would not propose to eliminate the other group's entitlements if it also meant the elimination of its own subsidies.

So let's return to a more balanced approach to welfare reform. How do we provide much needed assistance to those families desperately caught in the cycle of poverty without encouraging dependency? Let's dispel the myth of welfare queens driving their Cadillacs while they smirk at the system, and concentrate on the truly poor mothers simply needing a hand out of poverty. We know that if we don't support these families out of poverty, then they end up homeless on the streets.

We must provide these families with entitlements that encourage independence, subsidies tied to job development, and welfare linked to family protection. Surely, with the billions and billions of dollars spent every year, we could figure out a way to lift six million people out of poverty and homelessness.

Sadly, some people today approach a broken system by proposing more financial cuts. The skewed logic goes like this… if we cut people out of the system then we are forcing them to take care of themselves. Just like the mother bird forcing her offspring out of the nest to fly. Unfortunately, this sink or swim theory usually causes impoverished families to sink into life on the streets.

Proposing entitlement program cuts, however, continue to go on. Cut food stamps for hungry families because they just use them to buy alcohol; cut supplemental security insurance for the elderly and disabled, Medicaid for uninsured children, child nutrition programs, and welfare-to-work. The more we eliminate the more we force welfare queens out of their Cadillacs.

We keep up this approach to solving the welfare system going and we develop a growing pipeline of families ending up on the streets. Perhaps those who propose cuts to government entitlements are the same conspirators seeking to increase homelessness?

THIRTEEN

Bring On The War

I vividly recall one of the homeless residents living at PATH when I first started as the director. Jason (I changed his name) was a tall, well-built man filled with pride who became homeless after succumbing to a drug addiction. Although he continued to hold his head high, he also appeared uncomfortable if not embarrassed by having to resort to life in a homeless shelter.

He always seemed on edge, and quick to respond. A few brief informal talks with him, and I discovered he was a Vietnam war veteran who never quite got over the images he saw and the experiences he endured. Alcohol was his medicine of choice to soothe those images away.

After a month of working our program, Jason landed a job with a construction company and seemed to be doing well. Every week he met with his case manager, a fellow veteran, and talked about the issues in his life. After another month of work, his company had promoted him and even gave him a company car. Success, however, was as foreign to him as the people he was fighting against in the war. He just couldn't handle it.

So one night, he simply disappeared. He had abandoned his possessions that were still in his room, and deserted a program that had put him on a path to a healthy, self-sufficient lifestyle. Those of us on staff were both heartbroken and sad for him.

A few weeks later, we received a cryptic telephone call from Jason, telling us that he was back on the streets. The ghosts of war were stronger than the desire to succeed.

Sadly, Jason is one of a half a million veterans who become homeless each year in America. There appears to be a twisted link between homelessness and war.

If you want to increase homelessness, encourage our government to start a war. Many veterans who return from battle end up on our streets. In fact, there is a good chance that one of every four homeless adult males you see sleeping on the street, in a cardboard box, or on a bus bench had at one time served our country in the armed forces. It is a heart-wrenching, unacceptable statistic that should be a glaring, humiliating footnote to the problem of homelessness in our country.

Some time between being discharged from a military tour of duty and walking through the front door of a homeless program, homeless veterans by the thousands are falling through the cracks of our social system. We first praise them as heroes, throw elaborate parades with marching bands, and pat them on the back while later on when the balloons have deflated and the music stops, we turn our own backs against them redirecting our attention to more pressing issues.

Although we know that a majority of today's homeless veterans fought in Vietnam, this is not a Vietnam war syndrome. As more and more soldiers return home from more recent battles, they too encounter the same ghosts that most veterans face.

Could we not dispatch our own squad of rescuers to go behind the lines of homelessness to save every Private Ryan, every homeless veteran, caught in the trenches of hopelessness and despair? Where are the Tom Hanks of today seeking to rescue those postwar veterans dangling their lives between life and death scenarios on the streets of America? Certainly, saving homeless veterans should be a priority for our government!

The Post-traumatic Stress Disorder that many veterans take home from combat like a bad souvenir certainly messes people's state of minds. A recent veteran of the latest Iraq war commented to a local television reporter who had asked him how he felt when he saw the television news from the Iraqi battlefield. He said, "I listen to it, but I don't want to see it again. Some of that stuff I want to push away, and I don't want to talk about it."

The killing, the maiming, the utter violence of war is much worse than watching a Rambo movie or playing the latest violent Nintendo video game. Because in war, you can smell death, hear real screams and moans, and feel the reality of killing another person. You're not sitting on the couch in your comfortable middle-class suburban home while simulated violence is projected on your television. In battle, people do terrible things in order to survive, actions that would typically not occur on the streets of middle-class suburbia.

So you return home after a tour of duty on the battlefield experiencing nightmares and flashbacks. Your loved ones around you just can't relate to the images flashing across your memories. You detach yourself from those you love, many times allowing the ghosts of war to overcome the realities of life. You respond like the victims of rape, terrorism, or disasters who simply cannot forget the terrible images dancing in your head.

"What happened to my husband?" shout many wives receiving their war-torn spouses. No wonder many marriages break up and veterans detach and give up. Some commit the unthinkable. In the summer of 2002, a handful of veterans from the Afghanistan war returned home fighting the same demons that many other veterans encountered earlier. This time, however, the result was deadly. Four wives of veterans who had recently returned to their families were brutally killed by their husbands. Many other wives in the same situation accused their husbands of domestic violence. The ghosts of war came home with them.

Other veterans, however, do not resort to murder but instead choose alcohol or drugs to appease those terrible memories. They try to drink away their images because they have succumbed to the ghosts haunting their memories.

Many of those homeless men and women you see walking down our sidewalks of urban America arguing against imaginary foes just beyond the reach of their consciousness are still fighting those ghosts that perhaps have continued to trouble them for decades.

Where are the Ghostbusters when we need them? Could we not dispatch Bill Murray and Dan Aykroyd to trap every veteran's pesky ghosts and evil spirits so they can return home to life as it was before war? Let them pack up those ghost-busting contraptions and zap away the ghouls from every haunted veteran.

I wish it were as simple as that. Instead, our country needs to develop a more comprehensive system of preparing soldiers to return home. The Pentagon designs elaborate and effective campaigns for war—Operation Enduring Freedom, Operation Desert Storm, Operation Infinite Justice—why not Operation Healthy Veterans? We need to attack those ghosts that haunt our veterans so they can live with their families, emotionally healthy and able to reconnect to loved ones, and to not to resort to living on the streets.

If we're going to war, let's make sure we take care of those who risk their lives for our freedom by ensuring a healthy homecoming.

This is not an unpatriotic position. On the contrary, the most patriotic deed we could do is this—to guarantee that every soldier who puts on a uniform will be assured a place to go, provided help for emotional health, and assisted in re-connecting with loved ones, after serving his or her country.

If we fail in the effort to care for our veterans discharged from battle, every one of our war campaigns will simply be another human conduit into the pipeline of homelessness. More men and women will be spewed out of this conduit and succumb to life on the streets. Thank you very much for your military service, now here's your life…

Of course, this could be an intentional outcome for those scheming to increase homelessness. But we know better. To end homelessness means to also stop the flow of veterans becoming homeless.

Perhaps every war campaign should have Robin Williams as a military disc jockey lobbing joke after joke soothing the stress levels of our soldiers. Good morning, Vietnam! Good morning, Afghanistan! Good morning, Iraq! Perhaps even… Good morning, Homeless America!

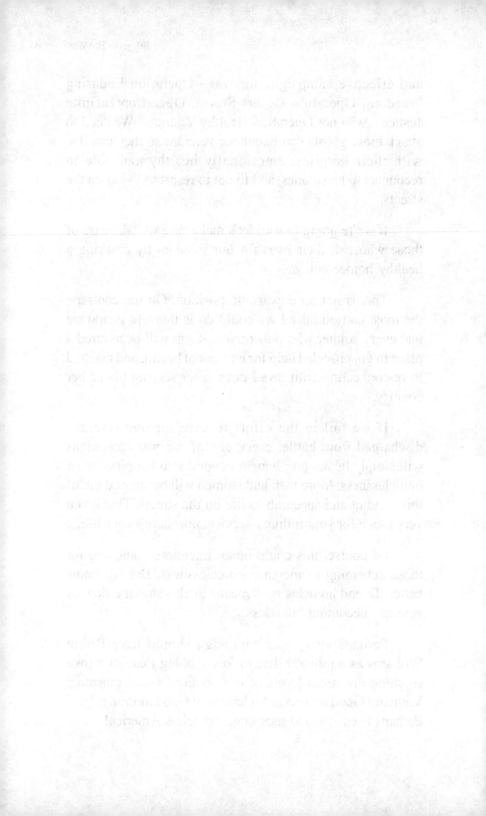

FOURTEEN

Free Will For The Mentally Ill

Her name was Margaret. She was a typical homeless woman pushing an old shopping cart overflowing with her life's possessions as she trekked through an upper-class neighborhood of Los Angeles filled with L.A.'s old moneyed families. She stood barely five feet tall and weighed a mere one hundred pounds. She was no threat to anyone except those who might feel she was a quality of life annoyance in a neighborhood wishing that all those homeless people would stop invading their tree-lined avenues, nicely groomed lawns, and sumptuously large homes.

Margaret Mitchell was an elderly woman who had been detached from her family for years, and ended up living on the streets. She was clearly overcome by phantoms lodged in her mental consciousness that haunted her very being. She strolled down the boulevard pushing her supermarket shopping cart when a couple of law enforcement officers on bicycles stopped her. They thought she might be possessing a stolen cart. The usual offense for a person who was homeless.

Being homeless, disoriented, and haunted by demons were her only crimes. But unfortunately, Margaret made a fatal mistake by reaching in her cart for a screwdriver. Why would she make such a threatening response with officers carrying arms, you might ask? Didn't she know that you don't make aggressive moves toward armed police officers? Easy for those of us who are mentally stable to say.

So the officers, obviously not following policy but feeling threatened nevertheless, pulled out their pistols and fatally shot the crazy woman. Her death caused an uproar among angry homeless activists who all along had felt that society had criminalized homeless people. Death is an inappropriate penalty for a homeless person trying to reach for a screwdriver in her cart. Candlelight vigils and angry marches marked this sad occasion.

I remember publishing a letter in the Los Angeles Times newspaper right after that incident wishing that one of PATH's street outreach teams, trained in dealing with mentally ill homeless people on the streets, would have been called to de-escalate the situation. That call never occurred, and tragically Margaret's life ended on that day in 1999.

Sadly, the actions of politicians nearly four decades earlier actually contributed to the cause of Margaret Mitchell's death. In the 1960's, California's state government decided to release residents of state-run mental health institutions by enacting a law called the Lanterman-Petris-Short Act that also gave people struggling with mental illness the civil right to make their own decision on whether they should be institutionalized. It obviously relieved the state of paying for this costly support of what many at that time called the 'warehousing' of people in need. But also, neither family member nor police officer could simply make the decision on whether to institutionalize a mentally ill person.

So those two police officers patrolling the streets of Los Angeles on their bicycles had no choice but to respond to this distraught homeless woman, rather than call mental health professionals to institutionalize her. Those limited choices became deadly.

Could it be that conspirators trying to increase homelessness started their dastardly deeds decades ago by releasing mental health patients and passing a law that only allowed re-institutionalization through self-induction? What a scheme. Like mentally ill persons are really going to say, "Stop, I am crazy, please institutionalize me!" It's a wicked way to increase homelessness.

It is a backward reality when those who are fighting for the civil rights of people battling crippling mental illness are actually keeping those who desperately need housing at arms length while they languish in alleys and sidewalks of our cities. It's absurd.

Many times, this downwardly mobile cycle results in incarceration. The Justice Department says that 16% of inmates in their system are mentally ill. Some say there are nearly 300,000 mentally ill inmates in our country's prison system.

Unlike most politicians who see advocating for solutions for homelessness as political death, Los Angeles County Sheriff Lee Baca has become a courageous public advocate in reforming the way our country deals with homelessness. Yes, a public law enforcement officer wanting to deal with homelessness! It's not an oxymoron. One factor that has motivated him is the dismal fact that his Los Angeles County Jail, the twin towers located outside of downtown Los Angeles, has become the largest mental health institute in the country with nearly 2,500 mentally ill inmates. It has become a revolving door, between Skid Row and jail, for homeless mentally ill people going from the streets to jail, back to the streets and again to jail. A depressing cycle of humanity carted around like a herd of disoriented cattle.

"The system is totally broke and the jails are not the answer," said Sheriff Baca to a local television reporter. A simple statement with powerful meaning. I'm sure those young rookie deputies just graduating from the sheriff's academy had no idea they would become mental health social workers.

So what is the answer? Lock up every mentally ill person we see on the street? Or respect their civil rights by allowing them to choose to be on the streets? There has to be a more civil approach than these two polarizing solutions.

In 2001, the California State Legislature indeed proposed a more sensible solution. The law was named after Laura Wilcox. I'm sure Laura would have never imagined that a landmark legal initiative aimed at helping mentally ill persons would actually be named after her. And given the reason why, I'm sure Laura would not have wanted the law to be named after her.

Laura was 19 years old when as an active, compassionate college student she decided to work at a public mental health clinic in Nevada City. Her decision was par for her young, but successful life. She had been valedictorian of her high school class, was active in student life at Haverford College, and was planning to work for a non-profit group.

On January 10, 2001 a middle-aged man walked into Laura's clinic carrying with him a history of fighting personal demons of delusional paranoia. He was convinced people were trying to kill him. His family could not sway him to take his medication or accept treatment, and watched in horror as he fell deeper and deeper into paranoia. He walked into Laura's clinic on that fateful day also carrying with him a gun. With his deranged logic he was there to even the score.

He fatally shot two clinic staff members including Laura. Her promising life tragically ended on that day at the hands of a disturbed man who battled evil spirits, and whose family had no control over his fate.

"Laura's Law", or AB1421, became a California state law in response to the many tragic events, such as Laura's death, at the hands of mentally ill persons. The law eliminates some of the barriers that previously prevented people who desperately needed mental health care from being institutionalized.

Laura Wilcox and Margaret Mitchell. Two completely different women falling victim to the same fate. Isn't it ironic? A young woman at the start of her promising adult life holding all the keys of society's success. An older woman struggling to survive on the streets of Los Angeles and battling personal demons with no promises, not even a shelter bed. One shot by a deranged mentally ill man, the other accidentally killed by a young police officer.

Sadly, these two women who never met and never knew each other fell prey to the polarizing groups who argued over whether mentally ill people have the civil right to live on the streets, to have their own control over whether they should be institutionalized.

Could it be that more sensible minds are now seeking to provide solutions, such as "Laura's Law"? That it takes the senseless death of two women positioned on different rungs of society's success ladder to force our community to respond more responsibly? Surely, those seeking to craft laws that result in the increase of homelessness would hope not.

But for the sake of future Laura's and Margaret's in our communities, let us hope common sense prevails over entrenched ideology.

FIFTEEN

At The Trough

Could a two-thousand-year-old-story have an impact on how our community responds to homelessness today?

That old Biblical tale of the man stripped, beaten and left for dead on the roadside near Jerusalem still shapes the way people respond to the homeless situation today. While religious leaders of that time walked by and ignored his plight, the man lying on the street was disregarded until a person from Samaria, a province of people who were despised and sworn enemies, stopped to give aid. This Good Samaritan story has been passed along from one generation to another ever since.

The account had been the answer to a simple question, "Who is my neighbor?" So who really is my neighbor, we might ask even today? Is it the Joneses living across the street nestled beyond their white picket fence? The Martinez family in the townhouse two doors down? The local barbershop at our nearest street corner? Or, as this story that was shared a couple of millenniums ago states—our neighbors are those who are in desperate need of our assistance.

This story haunts our urban streets from coast to coast. Because the man lying on the roadway from one town to another is no longer just one person in need of a Samaritan's help. Today, there are thousands and thousands of bodies sleeping in cardboard boxes, perched on bus stop benches or under bushes in our public parks, sleeping away their misery because people have lost hope in their redemption.

The story of the Good Samaritan, however, continues to inject a transfusion of hope into our society. It motivates people to spring into action, to do something, anything to help these sad people barely existing on the fringe of society.

So today faith groups and community groups, moved by the compassion and hospitality of a person who helped his enemy two thousand years ago, seek to help their neighbors in need. That's why we see benevolent groups set up outdoor soup kitchens in our local parks or streets, serving up piping hot meals to the homeless. The lines of hungry homeless people meander through our communities. The groups say it is their compassionate duty, using the Good Samaritan as their role model. Clearly, to feed a person who is hungry a nutritious meal must be God's work. No one should go hungry in our modern world today. It is a crime if we allow it.

And yet, is it a cold-hearted crime to ask the unthinkable? To dare ask if all of this compassion is really working, really helping these homeless people get off the streets? Some people actually think public feeding programs are simply enabling people to *stay* on the streets. In other words, it is increasing homelessness in our communities. Is this a dastardly thing to say? Or are these critics courageous people standing on the sidewalks shouting, "The Emperor has no clothes!"? Could the Good Samaritan story be just another secret initiative to increase homelessness?

Let's look at public feeding programs from a balanced perspective. If there are hungry people in our community, we certainly should pause from our daily activities to help them with compassionate acts. It is just the right thing to do at the right time. If that hungry person, however, returns to our soup kitchen counter day after day, should we not think beyond that simple delicious meal toward acts that will prevent her from becoming dependent on us for her every meal? I think so.

The critique of public feeding programs is that hungry people become dependent on these programs for their daily meals. These Good Samaritan, well-intentioned programs become another form of enabling people to stay homeless. So how do we feed hungry people without becoming enablers? How do we provide the fishing pole so that the homeless and hungry can catch their own fish, especially when "fish" are hard to catch in an urban environment cruel to those who can't keep up with today's fast-paced economy?

In the 1980's, then Secretary of the federal Housing and Urban Development department, Andrew Cuomo, termed the phrase "continuum of care" for services to the homeless. This continuum was to be a collaborative effort among community service providers to help transition a person who is homeless from living on the streets to accessing permanent housing. A homeless person participating in this continuum would theoretically be served by a street outreach case worker, enter an emergency housing program, access services to stabilize his or her condition, enter a transitional housing program linked to support services, and ultimately gain permanent affordable housing. At that time, HUD prioritized its funding allocations to service providers and communities who developed and participated in effective continuums of care.

A successful public feeding program that has a goal of passing out "fishing poles" rather than encouraging hungry people to be dependent on fish only, must link its program with the community continuum of care. These feeding programs could be the front door of the community system, encouraging people who are homeless to enter transitional programs that provide people with the tools to get off the streets—mental health care, substance abuse counseling, employment assistance, and housing. These programs would deter critics from pinning the enabling label on them as they pass out food while also linking people with services.

Feeding the homeless can very well be a compassionate duty without enabling the poor.

Unfortunately, some well-meaning Good Samaritan groups ignore this solution. People who are hungry, they say, have a right to be fed and do not have to be "forced" to access services. We should not control homeless people by making them do things that they choose not to do, they reason. If they want to eat, let them eat, barring any conditions.

I recall a few years ago that one public feeding program started passing out food to people who were homeless in a well-known park lined with million dollar homes that overlooked the Pacific Ocean. The community is a major attraction for tourists from all over the world. The neighbors yelled, "foul!" and tried to move the program away from the park and closer to social service facilities. But this group stayed put, stating, "These homeless people have the same right to eat food watching the sun set on the Pacific Ocean as the millionaires who live nearby."

So in the game of public feeding, the ante went up. From the right to be fed to the right to be fed with a view of the Pacific Ocean. It is amazing what people are willing to fight for.

Then there are the Good Samaritan groups that take feeding the homeless to another level. They put a price tag on the cost of the meal and literally sell that meal to the public who feel guilty that homelessness exists or who are compassionately moved to want to help people who are desperately hungry in our community. The newspaper ad reads: for $1.37 you can provide a piping hot slice of turkey on a serving of mashed potatoes and gravy, a delicious side of cranberry sauce and fluffy dressing, along with a scoop of ice cream with a cherry on top. It is a tangible way for the community to help the homeless. Especially during the holidays.

The photos of hungry children sitting next to their mother's who look sadly into the camera lens because they are unable to perform even one of the most basic functions of a mother—to feed her child—turn our hearts. And, by the way, open up our wallets as well. Literally millions flow into the coffers of these programs.

But does this really help the homeless? Or is it just another public feeding program—albeit one on marketing steroids—that provides compassionate services but enables people to stay at the trough day after day? These are questions that many Good Samaritan programs in our communities must ask themselves if they truly want to help the people they are feeding.

So many tough questions to be answered.

I don't think that the Good Samaritan who provided a simple good deed thousands of years ago would have ever imagined how complicated his simple act would become centuries and centuries later. But thank God, he didn't just walk by and ignore the man lying on the street.

SIXTEEN

NIMBYs R Us

Many of us are tempted to reminisce back to the good old days, when you could leave your front door unlocked and park your untethered bicycle in front of a store without worrying about someone snatching away your belongings. If only life could be so simple.

So we dream that our community and back yards become like Mister Rogers' Neighborhood. You can almost hear him singing, "It's a beautiful day in this neighborhood," as the chorus of make-believe neighbors join in, "…a beautiful day for a neighbor. Would you be mine? Could you be mine?…"

Yeah right. You can shut off that archaic 45 RPM record because those images just don't exist. Forget the make-believe neighborhood with the friendly police officer, local baker with the white hat, and the grandfatherly "Speedy Delivery" messenger. These characters are pure fiction.

Unfortunately, the yearning for Mister Roger's Neighborhood or a community like Leave It To Beaver's prompts people to fight tooth and nail to stop any social service program from invading their neighborhood. This knee-jerk response has become prevalent in both high end communities as well as neighborhoods suffering under the crush of poverty. Nobody wants them.

I remember when a community social service agency on Los Angeles' Westside wanted to place a homeless service center in a middle-class neighborhood. When the project came up to vote at the local city council meeting, hundreds of community members flooded the council chambers to testify against the project. Mothers screamed at the council members fearful that criminal elements would seep into the neighborhood. Their children were brought along to tell the leaders they would be afraid to walk on their streets to school if such projects were built. Business owners, homeowners, families, all fought to stop programs that would be helping people in need. The meeting lasted until two o'clock in the morning. The chorus was strong and vibrant… "Not In My Backyard!" It's the same choir as those who yearn to sing, "It's a beautiful day in this neighborhood…"

This typical NIMBY ("Not In My Backyard!") response is resonating within our communities, with reverberating affects of actually making the problem of homelessness worse. If there are no neighborhoods that will house homeless programs, how can we solve the problem? Perhaps the NIMBY attitude is another secret scheme to increase homelessness? It certainly pushes the emotional buttons of everyday people.

I, too, worry about my children walking in a neighborhood filled with drifters and people loitering on the streets. Who wouldn't worry? So when NIMBY advocates garner the support they need to prevent programs from starting, they use the highly emotional hot buttons that scare every parent of young children, every homeowner, every proprietor of business who aches for a neighborhood ruled by Mister Rogers. These buttons trigger waves of anger and fear—"when a homeless program enters your neighborhood, floods of rapists, child molesters, drug addicts, prostitutes, ex-convicts, and mentally ill wanderers will overwhelm your streets!" So say the hastily printed flyers and billboards that quickly spread throughout the community.

Who, in their right mind, would welcome this type of criminal element to the neighborhood anyway? The argument is stated quite clearly—homeless programs attract more homeless people. Take the homeless programs out of the neighborhood, and so go the homeless people.

Frankly, I just don't buy that. If you were homeless and living on the streets, where would you go? If I were living in Los Angeles in search of a place to sleep I would probably trek to the nearest beach, or find a hidden place along the freeway. Some community members living in Los Angeles' beach cities think NIMBY-ism is the way to solve homelessness. I tell them that if you really want to eliminate homelessness in your community, get rid of the beach, your beautiful weather, your clean parks. Then the people who are homeless would probably search for a better community in another part of town.

The problem with possessing a NIMBY attitude is that it is simply short-sighted. Yes, all of us want to protect our children from harmful people. That's a given. But to eliminate homeless programs is not the solution.

I realize that most of us work hard in trying to achieve the American Dream. We save our money for a down payment, we take on the daily grind of commuting to work, paying Uncle Sam's taxes, bringing home the bacon. Why? So that we can make a monthly payment that gives us that home with the white picket fence, curtains in the windows, and rooms filled with Ikea furniture. Home sweet home. Then years later, the value of this very personal asset starts to increase. Probably more than any other investment we might possess. It's an admirable dream. Reachable for many, but not all.

So why would we want to allow some new homeless shelter to move down the street, bringing the human residuals of their program with them, basically ruining our little nest egg of a neighborhood? We worked hard for what? For some program to shatter our dream?

Those hot buttons of emotions are certainly easy to push. It is not difficult to mobilize an angry community. The isolationist approach to protecting a neighborhood from outside elements is an easy sell for most people.

Ironically, neighborhood isolationist policies split both ways. On the one hand, communities battle social service agencies against the installation of any low-end projects that help the homeless or poor. On the other hand, advocates for the poor struggle with the wealthy to stop high-end projects from displacing people out of their communities. Isn't it strange that NIMBY-ism and gentrification are two peas in a pod?

We fight for the well-being of our communities, battling against low-end or high-end projects that might harm our residents. No homeless shelter! No youth center! No million dollar lofts! Homeless advocates were even picketing the opening of Los Angeles' Disney Hall. Give Disney's millions to the poor, not to a music hall for the rich!

What are we so afraid of that we're willing to speak out at a local city council meeting at one o'clock in the morning, that we're willing to picket along the red carpet of a civic project's grand opening? The tension of anger is caused by a simple push of our emotional buttons. It blinds us from seeing long-term solutions. Our near-sighted reactions actually do more harm than good.

Don't people understand that when a community prevents a homeless program from finding a home it is the same as stopping a homeless person from obtaining permanent housing and getting off the streets? Isn't this what we all want? To get people who are homeless off our streets!

Having no homeless people on the streets means our children can walk to school feeling safe and secure. It means people no longer have to sleep on unsafe and unclean Third World-like streets. Businesses no longer have to worry about panhandlers hitting up their customers. Developers would have the freedom to erect large high-end residential projects without worrying about displacing people living on the streets. Could we not describe such a community without homelessness as if it is Mister Rogers' Neighborhood?

The neighborhood of make-believe becomes a community of reality. This can only happen when the whole neighborhood takes responsibility for the cracks in our social safety net. We can tell those people who are trying to help the homeless to go away, to build their havens of service in another neighborhood. Or we can join together to fight poverty and homelessness so that everyone wins.

One possible solution could be patterned after the "Inclusionary Zoning Housing Ordinance." Communities are adopting these zoning ordinances (or land use policies) that encourage or mandate developers to include a certain percentage of their new residential developments (or their development budget) for low-cost, affordable housing. For example, in 2000, the city of Boston began requiring that 10% of new on-site residential units must be set aside for low-income, affordable housing units, or the developer must provide funding for these units in another project.

So why not develop an Inclusionary Zoning Ordinance for homeless projects? Why don't we put the burden of locating services in all communities, not just a few? Let the community know that until we solve the problem of homelessness, we must all suffer the consequences. Perhaps this would move people to action, move communities to fund and locate services that can solve the problem.

I know some people might think this suggestion is just another pipe dream from the neighborhood of make-believe. But if our communities continue the trend of embracing NIMBY-ism, the problem of homelessness will just get worse. We can't close our eyes and wish it to go away. We can't picket against the problem, scream and yell for it to disappear, and think that if we ban homeless programs from our neighborhood that homelessness will simply be solved. It won't be.

I wish we could welcome all new neighbors with an apple pie in our hands and a smile on our face, even those neighbors who set up poverty and homeless programs. Can you hear them singing, "Would you be mine, could you be mine?" But that, indeed, is probably a dream out of the world of make-believe. So let's forget the apple pie, the smiles, the corny children songs. How about if we just allow homeless programs to enter our neighborhoods without the verbal battles at the local city council chamber that last into the early morning hours?

The aura of Mister Rogers' Neighborhood is certainly more attainable if all neighborhoods worked together to solve the problem of homelessness rather than pawn the problem from one community to another. We may not all be wearing that light-colored buttoned sweater and singing those songs that attract children's attention, but we can hope for a real community that provides real solutions to homelessness.

SEVENTEEN

Bootstraps In An Age Of Sneakers

If you polled a group of middle class citizens in your city and asked them what they thought of that homeless person standing on the freeway off-ramp grasping a cardboard sign in search of handouts, at least half (if not more) would probably say he is just lazy and should go find a job. In fact, I've heard people holler outside their car windows with angry voices, while zooming by in the safety of their vehicle, "Go find a job, you lazy bum!" Just admit it, I'm sure you have thought of the same reaction while driving by a person who looks fit enough to deliver mail or at least flip hamburgers. While you commute to your daily grind of work, these people do nothing but beg for freebies. It's just not fair.

"Homeless people are lazy." say the critics. Why should we help them? Let them help themselves. With this perspective on solving homelessness—the don't-help-them-because-they-are-lazy viewpoint—homelessness would certainly increase. With no services helping people get off the streets, there would be more people homeless. Perhaps this is another quiet marketing campaign among those who really want to make the problem worse?

Let's look at this help-yourself campaign a little more closely.

People should just lift themselves up with their own bootstraps! What a concept for people who are homeless. Years ago, a bootstrap was a pair of loops inside the top rim of a heavy horse-riding boot. They were something to pull on when you shoved your foot into the boot, something to help get your ankle past the inside heel.

A two hundred year old story described some baron who allegedly pulled himself and his horse out of the mud by pulling on his own hair. One hundred years later, the story was changed to the baron pulling himself and his horse out by the bootstraps. It's just like the old game of telephone where you whisper in a person's ear, "The horse rider is taking the lazy way home." Then after the sentence is whispered over and over from one person's ear to another, by the time the last person hears it, he hears, "To get a real house the homeless can't be lazy."

So today, we say that people who are homeless should just lift themselves up with their own bootstraps. Think about that again. Do the laws of physics allow someone who is weighted down by his own heavy boots to pull himself up by tugging on them? It's just not physically possible.

Yet we shout out of our moving SUV's, down to the desperate people holding tattered signs for help, demanding that they do something that is physically unrealistic, "Get a job! Lift yourselves up with your own bootstraps! You don't need anybody else's help!"

Like that's going to really work. And if you focus more on that person who is homeless standing on the street corner, you may see that he isn't even wearing shoes! Now we really have put our logic in a pickle. How can someone lift themselves up with their own bootstraps, when they are not even wearing boots!

Making unrealistic demands on the poor and homeless is not the answer to ending homelessness. Lifting yourself up with your own bootstraps is more myth than solution.

To make matters worse, riding boots are out and sneakers are in. We live in an age of sneakers where most of the world is running full speed, just to keep up with the pace of society. Life is a constant sprint from one job to another, juggling mortgages and the spiraling costs of middle-class living, keeping relationships intact, and insuring your kids have that *Home Improvement* upbringing. We could never keep the balls in the air with mere riding boots. We would trip and fall through the cracks of successful living, and God forbid, end up homeless like those bums on Skid Row alley.

So Nikes are a necessity. Now go to your local Footlocker sneaker outlet and price the latest athletic footwear. If you haven't bought high end Adidas in a decade or more, you'll be floored at the three figure price tags. Then again, years ago we would be choking on our percolator-brewed coffee, if we knew we would be buying four dollar cups of latte on our way to work every day.

The age of sneakers is an expensive endeavor where only the economically fittest can compete. And we tell the poor and homeless to lift themselves up with their bootstraps?

I grew up being taught that hard work counts, where the cream of the hard-working crop of people rise to the top. You work hard, pay your dues, stay in school, stay out of trouble, and the road to middle class successful living is full of green lights.

I always thought the game of success had fair rules. In a contest there should always exist a level playing field. But what if you went to Fenway Park and saw one baseball team with six outfielders and the other team with only two? What if you went to a Laker basketball game, and their team had eight-foot high baskets while the other team's baskets were twelve-foot high? It just wouldn't be fair. We fans, let alone the players, would not allow such lop-sided competition.

But in the game of life, the rules are different. Life isn't fair. If you've been thrown out of your house because your spouse was using you as a punching bag or if you never had a family environment that encouraged education, you don't have the same tools to succeed in life's competition. If you grew up in a community where guns and drugs were much more prevalent than books and calculators, the odds against your success are higher. Sure, some people make it, but most don't.

Some of us grow up with every opportunity in the world, and some of us have nothing. What an insult it must be when those who drive by in luxury cars—a simple result of an education or middle class up-bringing provided by their parents' hard work—spit at the feet of homeless people who were raised with no opportunities at all. "Get a job! Lift yourself up with your own bootstraps!" Is this justice?

If the real game of life was fair, we should all have the same opportunities. I once lived in an impoverished orphanage as an infant in a large Asian metropolis, with no family, no education, no one encouraging me to succeed. I wish I could say that I arrived at my current status because I lifted myself up with my own bootstraps. But that is just not the case.

I was adopted into a middle class American family in Long Beach, California where I was given every opportunity to make it. I was surrounded by an environment of love, an education that empowered me, a safe neighborhood, and a future that was always painted brightly. Without opportunity, I could have ended up living on the streets of an Asian city rather than gaining a post-graduate degree and writing a book. Someone—in this case my family—lifted me up, bootstraps and all, and provided me with tools of opportunity to succeed. Justice worked for me.

Unfortunately, justice does not rule the streets. How can kids discharged from foster care, women expelled from abusive homes, men raised in violent neighborhoods, really lift themselves up out of poverty and homelessness? The odds are against them.

We have to change the rules of the game. Assuming everyone is just lazy and should make it on his own is a cruel approach to a complex problem. Instead we need to arm those who have fallen through the cracks of society with sneakers that allow them to run in the game. Creating safe and secure environments, equipping people with the tools to find and keep a job, helping people overcome life-threatening addictions, debilitating mental or physical illnesses, are the real Nikes for success.

Let us dispel the myth of bootstraps, and empower people with tools of opportunities. They can run if they bare sneakers that protect their feet, if the road ahead is smooth, if the wind of encouragement is at their back.

No more insults screaming from our car windows. As if our shouts of discouragement are really going to make a difference. The man standing at the freeway off-ramp needs tools of opportunities, not disparaging remarks. He needs sneakers to run the race, not bootstraps to pull himself up. He needs people who want to end homelessness, not increase it.

EIGHTEEN

Give Them Liberty, Not Death

A group of business people from China was on an official visit to Los Angeles, hosted by a local public official. Sporting cameras and inquisitive questions on the state of this world-class city, they met with Los Angeles business leaders, stopped off at some of the city's famous sites, and then ended up traveling through its downtown Skid Row area. Like most first-time visitors to this infamous cluster of street blocks packed with encampments of homeless people, they were shocked. Their cameras whirled and their barrage of questions began. "How can the richest country in the world allow its people to live in such abject poverty on the streets?"

The local official's response was simple. "America is a free country. We allow our people the freedom to choose to live this way." Clearly, these visitors were not convinced that our country is committed to helping the poorest of our citizens. The images were much more graphic and telling than words from a local politician. So this Chinese delegation continued to snap more and more pictures ready to take home incriminating evidence that our country isn't exactly what is projected in the movies.

Sadly, some people resonate with this public official's perspective on homelessness. Homeless people have the freedom to choose what they want to do. If they choose to live on the streets or in some grimy urban alley, that is their choice. They are free; our country is free. What is the problem?

Have we cheapened the meaning of freedom in this country? I think we are confusing the freedom to live on the street with our country's perspective on the freedom of speech, religion, the press, to bear arms. Why not add the freedom to live in squalid conditions on the street? If that's the case, why not add the freedom to play on the freeway, to jump off roofs, to let our children play with loaded guns?

We are a free country where the tired, the poor, the huddled masses swarmed to the land of the free by the thousands. And when they trekked through Ellis Island they saw the Statue of Liberty, where engraved on the pedestal is Emma Lazarus' famous "huddled masses" words, including, "Send these, the homeless, tempest-tost to me." We are a people of liberty with welcoming arms to those in need, including the very homeless who we have allowed to squander their lives away on our streets. Isn't it ironic that we have welcomed the homeless and poor from other countries, and at the same time given our own home-grown homeless the freedom to live like animals?

There is something wrong with this picture. Freedom is more precious than simple words that allow people to flounder on the streets.

At the twilight of the American Revolution, Patrick Henry's words of freedom, "Give me liberty or give me death!" rang out to those yearning for a free country, encouraging young revolutionaries to bear arms and fight for liberty. They were fed up with foreign rule and were willing to die for this urgent cause.

A couple of hundred years later, we give homeless people liberty and freedom to live on violent, filthy streets that could very well cause their death. But are these people without homes dying because they want the freedom of outdoor living? (And we are not speaking of lawn chairs, sunglasses, and margaritas here.)

It is that myth of choice again... but it is a faulty myth; homeless people do not choose to be homeless. If so, then perhaps they are choosing their own death, like our country's first freedom fighters. But to be thrown out of your house by an abusive spouse, to lose your job because of downsizing or become sick without health insurance, are not choices. To be unable to afford permanent housing because your minimum wage barely allows you to feed and clothe yourself, is not a choice.

Homelessness is not a choice. The woman and child sleeping in a parked car out of sight from every day people are not shouting, "Give me liberty or give me death!" They are quietly pleading, "Give me a roof over my head, and a safe place for my child to grow up." To assume that homeless people are freedom fighters, struggling for the cause of liberty is just wrong. They are not choosing to live in squalor, as if it is an American right. Rather, they are struggling for the right to shelter and food.

Homelessness becomes a civil right issue where people are in need of social justice and equality. The basic rights of housing, food, health care, protection from violence are at stake here.

Forty years ago, Martin Luther King Jr. stood on the steps of the Lincoln Memorial dreaming beyond the injustices of his day. He shouted out to the masses who huddled around the reflecting pool on Washington's Mall,

"Let freedom ring!" His words had a rallying affect on the tired, poor, and huddled masses craving for soothing words and changed ways that would bring justice to the forefront of society. Freedom from discrimination and injustice meant people of all races and religions would join together and embrace the rights of others.

Yet today we have skewed these words of freedom. Sadly, the tired, poor, and huddled groups of homeless people surviving on our streets only hear words of freedom that simply allow them to sustain their hopeless lives. These words ring in their ears like an annoying high-pitched sound, "You have the freedom to live on the streets. You have the right to be homeless." This is not liberty that Patrick Henry and his freedom fighters fought for before the birth of our country. It is not freedom that Martin Luther King Jr. dreamed about in our nation's capital.

We should not be giving people the freedom or liberty to live in destitute conditions. We are simply chaining people to a life of poverty. That downward spiral of homelessness starts with low-paying jobs, no health insurance, and volatile home lives. Then when people hit the sidewalks after falling off of society's success ladder, we simply tell them that they chose this state of life, that they have the freedom to live this way.

What a way to increase homelessness. Blame the problem on the very people who are affected.

It's your choice, we tell that man sleeping on the streets. Hidden behind door number one is a house with a white picket fence and a secure job in a blue chip company. Or choose door number two, a tattered cardboard box perched on Skid Row where your only job for the day is to line up at the local soup kitchen for the day's meal. Choose one or two, two or one. The decision you make is your responsibility. This is what freedom is all about. What a great country we live in!

But what if we look at this a different way? Let's swap lenses. What if people are not choosing to walk through that door, but instead are being shoved through the door? Those human pipelines to homelessness pass through these doors of life without giving a person an opportunity to choose door number one. It becomes a cruel game of success where the losers end up on the streets, perhaps even facing death. Then we taunt them by pointing a blaming finger at them.

What chains must we cut in order to free people from homelessness? Rather than giving people the freedom to live on the streets, we should be giving people the freedom to get off the streets.

Let's open doors for people who feel every door of opportunity is locked. Let's open the doors of employment, healthcare, affordable housing, personal counseling, and safe neighborhoods. So people will truly be liberated from the chains of homelessness. Give them liberty, not death.

Then when people from other countries visit us, they will be taking pictures of our proud national treasures and entertainment venues. Their souvenirs will not be snapshots of national neglect.

Let's dream like Martin Luther King Jr. Wouldn't it be wonderful for people living on the streets to shout to our community, "Free at last! Free at last! Thank God Almighty, I am free at last!"

NINETEEN

Give It Up

There is an ironic phenomenon occurring in our community today towards homelessness. While many people living on the streets have simply given up on life, convinced that their destiny is an existence languishing in alleys and parks, those of us who are housed living in middle-class havens have also given up on ever finding solutions to ending the plight of homelessness. For decades, homelessness has gnawed at our society, eating away at our determination to resolve it. So, now, after years and years of seeing those men standing at our freeway off-ramps grasping on to tattered cardboard signs, responding to those newspaper appeals to "feed the hungry", and supporting good-intentioned service agencies, we have succumbed to sheer tiredness.

Compassion fatigue has overcome us. Just like the man sleeping under a freeway bridge tired of playing in the game of success, we are tired of enduring the effects of homelessness on our community and supporting the causes. How many more of those photos of grinning homeless people sitting in front of a hot-turkey meal can we bear? How many more stories of impoverished American children—at least there are no photos of bloated stomachs—can we read about? How many more rubber-chicken fundraising dinners can we consume? How many more panhandlers can we ignore?

Could it be that the clandestine campaign to increase homelessness is behind all of this? Get people to simply throw their arms up in the air in resignation, and the problem gets even worse.

It used to be that people would embrace the idea of helping homeless people. Now, communities rally against services moving into their neighborhoods. It used to be that people would freely write a check in support of homeless services. Now, they are more worried about earning their own paycheck. Where there was compassion, there is now indifference, sometimes even hostility.

Yet I know we have not completely lost our sense of compassion. Look at the amazing response to giving to the families affected by the 9-11 disaster. But a one-time tragedy is so different than a decades-old problem that, in fact, seems to be increasing. Fighting homelessness in this environment feels like trying to stop a Midwestern flood using a small plastic bucket. We can scoop and scoop the water out as fast as we can, but the flood of water just keeps growing.

Why are we tired? Why do we want to give up?

Like any conflict, there comes a point when we tire of funding constant battles—especially if it appears we are losing. The American government, today, spends one billon dollars every year in the fight to end homelessness. When you add private funding that supports homeless services, there is a lot of money being spent to help those living on the streets. You would think with all of that funding, we could end homelessness. But if you polled the average urban citizen, most people would say the problem seems to be getting worse. Are we ready to give up because we think homelessness is a lost cause?

Some people who are ready to concede defeat might quote Jesus when he stated, "You always have the poor with you." Should we resort to the fact that we will always have the homeless with us? If that is truly the case, why do anything? Just give up.

Paul Tepper, the Executive Director of the *Institute For The Study of Homelessness and Poverty* based in Los Angeles, once described to me how the community responds to homelessness. He said that people react in three ways: anxious, angry or apathetic. We can be *anxious* over the fact there are homeless people in our community, worried for our children or even worried for the people living on the streets. Some of us become *angry* that people are loitering in our parks and streets, panhandling and intimidating hard working citizens. These are the people rallying against homeless services and encouraging law enforcement to sweep the homeless out of the community.

Then there are those in our community who are *apathetic*. They are resigned to the fact that homeless people will just be a part of the community. There is nothing they can do so they have just given up.

I would add a fourth community response—*action*. We can be anxious, angry, or apathetic, but neither of these responses will resolve the problem of homelessness. If our community, however, is moved to action, amazing solutions can occur.

During the 1980s, popular fads swept our country— friendship bracelets, break dancing, boom boxes and Rubik's cube, to list a few. This was also a decade when homelessness seemed to be out of control in our country. Few people took notice of the many groups of community people who decided to take action. They met in church basements, school classrooms, community rooms, and in living rooms. They planned, dreamed, and prayed for solutions to homelessness.

The Los Angeles area is a good example of how communities responded to homelessness. The decade of the 1980s birthed dozens of homeless agencies that started programs to assist homeless families, to build permanent affordable housing, to provide HIV/AIDS services, healthcare, and transitional housing. Today, these agencies have become local and national leaders in fighting homelessness. They continue to be on the front lines, providing lifesaving services and standing up for the rights of people who have no homes. They are the hope for a better future.

Fatigue is common. Especially when we are in a fight for saving lives. But giving up cannot be an option. While many of those living on the streets have decided to quit making their lives better, we cannot give up in our quest to empower them.

Let's give it up for those fighting homelessness, but not consider giving up on this important, life-sustaining cause.

TWENTY

An Extreme Machine

He was an odd person to play the role of peacemaker. Encounters with law enforcement dogged his existence. Especially that dreadful encounter on March 2, 1991 when Rodney King was pulled over by four white Los Angeles police officers. The city woke up the next morning watching videotape on the morning news shows of four officers physically beating down this black motorist with swinging batons and angry kicks.

A year later, a sympathetic jury from a local suburb acquitted these same officers from their obvious crimes. The infamous verdict caused a horrific race riot throughout Los Angeles where 55 people died, almost 2,400 were injured, and nearly one billion dollars of damages transpired. One race attacked another. Unwieldy street gangs assaulted business owners protecting their property. Cars were torched and buildings trashed. Extremists prevailed on the streets.

While the riots besieged the city, a shocked and overwhelmed King was quoted on television saying, "Can't we all just get along?" They were impromptu words by a man who unintentionally spoke words of peace in a literally war-torn American city.

Today, those words should be spoken again as community groups fight over the issue of homelessness.

Once again, extremist groups dominate the discussion, preventing any reasonable solutions to surface from the choppy waters of the community's response to homelessness.

It's rough out there. Try convincing a protective homeowners association to support a local homeless shelter in their neighborhood. Mom's toting their infants in strollers will come out in droves. Try persuading a Business Improvement District that laws protecting a homeless person's right to sleep in front of their stores is good. The wealthy business people will form Political Action Committees and seek to install their own local politicians sympathetic to the business community. Try asking a homeless advocacy group to support ordinances that ban homelessness on the streets. Marches and candlelight vigils will overwhelm the streets before you could even drive home today.

Homelessness has become an emotional, polarizing issue that is splitting our communities. Groups possessing their own highly-charged, very personal views on this issue are digging into their trenches, not willing to budge. In a Los Angeles beach community one neighborhood group started taking candid photos and videos of homeless people drinking in alleys, walking deranged on the streets, and even using the gutters as bathrooms. They put these images on public viewing through the web and at local city council meetings. Their intent—project fear and disgust into the debate.

A perfect mode of operation for those seeking to increase homelessness in our community. Let the extremists dominate the debate.

Sadly, we are falling into this trap of fighting one another, rather than resolving this dreadful problem of homelessness. Police departments are pushed by the community to shove the homeless population into other neighborhoods. Advocacy groups picket urban renewal projects, as if renewing a neighborhood block is a bad thing. Local residents shriek at city council members when homeless agencies want to move in. Businesses hire their own private security teams to police their own neighborhoods. This vigilante response to people who have no place to call home is a strange, extreme reaction.

There is an old saying that when elephants fight, the grass gets trampled. When those in power fight one another, the little people get hurt. As our communities continue to rev up their extreme machines, fighting one another, pointing accusing fingers at each other, and screaming their viewpoints on rooftops and editorial pages, the very people who really need help get trampled. They resort to life in an alley. Life without a home.

Some even get shot.

Improving communication and trust among elephants is a good first step toward resolving homelessness. Because some elephants are from Mars and others are from Venus. Some elephants are "Mr. Fix-its" who "go to their caves" to sort things out on their own when they are upset. Others run the "Home Improvement Committee" who "go to the well" when they need emotional cleansing. If John Gray, of the "Men Are From Mars, Women Are From Venus" fame can convince two opposing sexes to improve their relationships and actually have a harmonious, loving existence, why can't community groups do what Rodney King asked—can't we all just get along?

Protecting one's own group at the expense of another is not a good solution. If every neighborhood's attitude were to "build your shelter anywhere else but here," there would be no place to house people who are homeless. The problem just gets worse. If every police force, pressured by political and community elephants, swept the homeless out of their communities, there would be no place for homeless people to go. The problem gets worse. If every homeless advocacy group that believed homeless people have the right to sleep, eat, panhandle on the streets, and use the streets as their own restroom, were to control local laws, our communities would be a mess.

Let's dismantle the extremist's machine and begin a dialogue between opposing forces. The ironic factor in this debate on homelessness is that every group really possesses the same goal—to no longer have homeless people on our streets. This common aim is the light at the end of the tunnel. We simply disagree on how to get through the tunnel. So we fight and fight against one another, screaming and yelling, picketing and politicking, pushing and shoving, until we finally are all stuck in the darkness of the tunnel.

If we bring the "Martian" and the "Venusian" groups working together as one to get through this dark tunnel of homelessness that ravages our communities, we could actually get to the other side. From darkness to light. From homelessness to being home.

We just need someone—anyone—to keep shouting to us all, "Can't we all just get along?"

TWENTY-ONE

Imagine

Could there really be a clandestine group of conspirators perched in glass office towers high above our urban centers pushing and pulling levers that control the flow of homelessness into our country? Talk about an extremist perspective on the state of homelessness in our country today! Can this be one? Yet some people believed the world was flat until Christopher Columbus dispelled that myth. A perfect example of how we sometimes confuse fact with myth.

So would imagining that there exists an evil group of connivers seeking to increase homelessness in our country be a simple myth or fact? On the surface, such a group of evildoers certainly appears to be an absurd legend that only leftist extremists would probably assume. On the other hand, try explaining to a foreign visitor why the richest and most powerful country on earth allows citizens to languish in Third World conditions on its streets and alleys. If I were the foreign tourist in America, I would certainly snap souvenir photos of Skid Row America as evidence for those back home who might doubt my description. Because people living on the streets of America seem to be an absurd anomaly that only snapshots in living Kodak colors would prove that homelessness in America is a fact, not a myth.

All the various perspectives, responses, and actions toward homelessness described in this book—from a downward spiral of affordable housing to wages that keep low-scaled workers poor; from outlawing homelessness to turning a blind eye to the mentally ill; from shoving homeless people out of a community to fostering homeless youth; from ignoring those who fight for our country to simply giving up on all solutions—provide glimpses of a mythical Oliver Stone conspiracy that we simply can not quickly dispel as absurd. The existence of homelessness is like having all of society's bad omens occur at once, like having every unhealthy star in the social safety net universe be in alignment tearing giant holes in the net that allow people to fall.

Our communities lack the vision to see beyond the frontlines of homelessness. If we know that we have more people than houses to accommodate them, shouldn't we build more affordable dwellings? If we know that eighteen-year-old emancipated foster youths are not ready to take on the adult role of finding permanent employment and independent living, shouldn't we provide for them? If we know that mentally disabled individuals do not have the capacity to ask for help, shouldn't we make the decisions for them? If we know that a quarter of our homeless population fought in a previous war, shouldn't we prepare our veterans before they are discharged from service?

If we know... shouldn't we have the vision and courage to do something about it?

Perhaps resignation has overwhelmed any sense of vision. We are resigned to the fact that the homeless will always be here. As long as they stay within the confines of their Skid Row neighborhood, giving up seems to be the easiest option.

"As long as they clear them out before I move into that million dollar loft. As long as that homeless shelter is in a neighborhood other than mine. As long as homelessness does not affect me, then let's move on to bigger and more pressing issues."

I cannot imagine this being the final resolution.

What do I tell that elderly homeless woman, strapped in her rickety wheel chair knocking on the glass door of our homeless program at six o'clock at night needing a place to stay? What do I tell that man who spent years of his life serving in our armed forces but now is overcome by the ghosts of war? What do I tell that young mother who holds her infant child in her arms whispering her pleas of help to our social workers? Their personal testimonies are not human myths; they are real stories. This is not text for the next direct mail appeal for money. These real people are a result of a broken down system of care, a community that lacks vision, a society filled with extreme positions.

Someone needs to imagine a better future for them.

We need more prophets in our society that will stand up to the decision makers and stalwarts of our communities, to tell them not to give up on the people lingering on our streets. No more excuses that these people are lazy and caught up in their own destiny. No more myths that they are Welfare Queens taking advantage of the system.

We need our community leaders to imagine a better place for our people in need. A kitchen and living room, a bedroom and bathroom. A neighborhood with a safe school for our children, and a local store overflowing with fresh food. A permanent job with a wage that allows us self-sufficiency. A community that has no more people sleeping on our streets.

Actually, these are tangible images. It does not seem too difficult. But all these issues and extreme positions, laws and ordinances, broken systems and neglect, myths and ineffective programs, seem to cloud the problem. Through the fog of community neglect and infighting, it is hard to imagine a street without homeless people when so much of these cluttering issues block our creativity and energy. We are all stuck in that dark passageway, caught in a traffic pileup, unable to see the light at the end of the tunnel. We need to clear our vision so that we can imagine a better future for our community, especially those who are floundering.

Someone needs to imagine a better future.

I still remember where I was when John Lennon was shot on December 8, 1980. I can also remember the music that the television and radio stations played days after. It was his popular song, "Imagine." As if his death might prompt the world to imagine a better society, a better community for all. Of course, he proposed no heaven, no hell, no borders, no religion, and no possessions. Not a particularly balanced approach to a better society. But the extremity of his lyrics was poignant. The song makes a powerful point.

Perhaps if Lennon were still living today, he might have rewritten his song to provide hope for those languishing on the streets, for a community overwhelmed, and for leaders paralyzed into inaction. Can you imagine what his lyrics might say?

Imagine there's no hunger
It's easy if you try
No hard sidewalk below us
Above us no more sky
Imagine all the people
Living for today

Imagine there's no abuse
It isn't hard to do
Nothing to hurt or scare us
And no more insults too
Imagine all the people
Living life in peace

Imagine no unemployment
I wonder if you can
No more need for begging
Just a community filled with love
Imagine all the people
Sharing all the world

You may say I'm a dreamer
But I'm not the only one
I hope someday you'll join us
And the world will live as one

TWENTY-TWO

Hunting For Good Will

Imagining a better world is more than simple music lyrics that a generation of Beatle fans can sing. A better world means real steps on a road that can be politically risky, filled with potholes and barriers.

In order to travel on the path of overcoming homelessness it takes a strong-willed society—a community that is willing to face risky political polls, prepared to invest money even during bad economic times, ready to stand up to NIMBY groups, and amenable to change government programs that are stuck in bureaucratic ways.

I sometimes think our communities are like Will Hunting, the genius janitor at MIT played by Matt Damon in the movie, *Good Will Hunting*. It is the story of this young working-class kid who is smarter than the professors but is resigned to the fact that his fate in life is to be a janitor or bricklayer. He chooses the road to self-destruction when those who care about him seek to steer him toward understanding his gifts. His childhood friend in the movie, played by Ben Affleck, tells him, "You're sitting on a winning lottery ticket. It would be an insult to us if you're still around here in twenty years."

I look at our communities today and see the same. They are filled with genius educators, entrepreneurial businesspeople, creative problem solvers, hard working social service providers. And yet, despite the giftedness that our communities possess we seem to be on a path of self-destruction regarding our response to homelessness. We can't seem to understand that we have the power within ourselves to overcome this societal blight. We are sitting on a winning lottery ticket that could pave the way for a clean street with no homelessness. Wouldn't it be an insult if homelessness were still around here in twenty years?

It all comes down to will. The old saying is true today—if there is a will, there is a way. No more excuses. If we really want to end homelessness, we could. That is why the assumption that there might be a secret group of conspirators working to increase homelessness is not a far-fetched left-wing theory. When you look at the big picture, you can see that our communities have the resources, talent, ideas, and ability to end homelessness. We are just missing one ingredient—we don't have the will.

We need more political leaders who have the vision to buck the norm. To push for more affordable housing and homeless services, even in neighborhoods that reject them. The will of our public leaders carry weight. Can they carry the cause of overcoming homelessness to a weary and wary public? If they allow opinion polls and campaign donors to dictate their vision, then our cause is lost. But if they take the high road of seeking to eliminate homelessness in our communities at any cost, then political will has triumphed.

Self-preservation is a tempting goal for public figures. Stay away from controversial political issues and stick to filling potholes in the street. Then re-election is a certainty. But the famous political leaders that we learn about in our history books were the ones who had the courage to see past the latest opinion poll and the vision to pursue bold causes—to end slavery, to fight Communism, to send a man to the moon. Which leaders might be the ones who embrace another bold cause—to eliminate homelessness?

What about the will of our business community? They benefit the most when homelessness has ended. No more haggard beggars pestering their customers. Gone are the intoxicated men hanging out on the street corner outside of their shops. A clean and secure neighborhood means more bucks in their pockets. You would think that the business community would be tripping over each other excited to support services that help homeless people get off the streets. And yet, in the past few years America's businesses only donated .01% of its pre-tax profits to charity.

In this era of Enron, Worldcom, and even Martha Stewart, Corporate America has an opportunity to flex its charitable muscles and show our country their will to end homelessness. When it comes to charity, Apple Computer must "Think Different," Ford should act with "No Boundaries," Nike could "Just Do It," and Corporate America must truly make a difference. Because when homelessness ends, the community benefits and business profits.

How about the philanthropic community? Giving goes in cycles. One year the funding priority went to AIDS programs, another year to children's education, another for breast cancer. A couple of decades ago, homelessness was the flavor of the month. But like a child distracted into playing another video game, people have moved on to other causes. Homelessness is no longer the sexy Hollywood charity cause. It has been twenty years since the spike of the number of homeless people occurred in our country. And yet, today what has changed? Homelessness still ravages our communities. So it is harder today to find a donor for homeless services than it was ten to twenty   years ago.

We also need the support of the faith community. Insulated behind their walls of worship are the very people we encounter each day at our work place, schools, and neighborhoods. They reflect the resources and talent in our community.

The faith community also offers a light for a world that battles darkness, especially on our streets. The fight to overcome homelessness is more than a physical battle, it is also spiritual. People living on our streets need hope. They, too, need to be able to see the light at the end of the tunnel and have the vision to overcome their personal demons, their life's barriers. The will of the faith community has a powerful impact on changing people's lives.

Where there is a will in our community, there is a way. A way to end homelessness.

Every four years, our country has an awesome national ritual that at times rivets the attention of our people. Bumper stickers sprout up, banners fly, advertisements air, news shows are dominated by talking heads and masses of junk mail flood our homes. It is the time to elect a president.

In most normal election cycles the losing candidate concedes the race on the night of the first Tuesday in November. In front of thousands of tired and disappointed supporters, and the glare of television cameras that broadcast images to millions around the country, the candidate makes his concession. In almost every speech, the candidate says, "The people have spoken. Their will has been revealed." It is an acknowledgement, not only of the people's will, but also of the power of our community's will.

Somehow we need to garner this same will, harnessing the energy and resources of the people in our country to undertake another bold social initiative—to end homelessness in America. Can we, the people, speak our will like we do every four years in a presidential election? Can we overcome our weariness toward the overwhelming problem of homelessness that devastates our community? Yes, we are tired of encountering this shameful blight in our neighborhoods. Perhaps we are even tired of donating our money to a cause that never seems to go away. Can we rise up from this weariness?

Can we also overcome our wariness over our community's infighting among mistrustful groups? Talk radio, newspaper editorials, and local public meetings are filled with extremists pointing accusing fingers at each other, fighting to make their positions heard. We scream and accuse to the point that we forget that our energy toward "saving" our neighborhoods or strengthening our positions could be used to resolve the problem. Can we all just get along?

We are a powerful and mighty country because the people in our communities are amazingly gifted. Let us not take the path of community self-destruction. There is a lot at stake.

Can we, together, raise our voices, our votes, our money, our resources toward the elimination of homelessness? Then we all could proudly say—"The people have spoken!"

Epilogue

At times, I have traveled with our street outreach teams who are compassionate and determined case workers that work with people living under freeway overpasses, in abandoned buildings, and parks throughout Los Angeles. They provide basic necessities for homeless people and encourage them to enter a formal homeless program. I remember walking on a dirt path along the side of the 101 Freeway near Hollywood among the overgrown brush that stood taller than me. Except for the sound of cars zooming by, it almost felt like we were in a jungle.

After ten minutes of walking, the brush partially opened up to reveal a small cardboard encampment under a freeway bridge. A half a dozen homeless people were living in these squalid conditions hidden from the view of passing cars or from any local street. I was shocked. Once again I was viewing a scene that resembled a squatter community in a Third World nation.

Our broken system of care for people who live on the lowest rung of our society has forced people to seek shelter in extreme conditions. They hide from the dangers of the street and seek shelter from the elements. Our system has failed them.

Today, however, there is hope. Two movements in our country will have a powerful effect on ending homelessness, if the will of the people supports them.

The first is the "Housing First" campaign. Spearheaded by the National Alliance To End Homelessness and cutting-edge agencies like Beyond Shelter in Los Angeles, this movement is challenging the paradigm of homeless services.

Two basic aspects of this strategy are:

(1) Re-house people who are homeless into permanent housing as fast as possible. In other words, don't let them flounder in emergency and transitional housing programs too long when they could be in their own independent living situation.

(2) Provide supportive services through housing assistance and follow-up case management that will help people who have accessed permanent housing stay off the streets.

The key to the success of this approach is ensuring that a community has enough permanent affordable housing for everyone. So the push within this movement is for communities to focus homeless service resources toward increasing the housing stock linked with supporting case management services.

A second movement within our country that is just starting to take shape is the development of "strategic collaborations" among non-profit service agencies. As I talk to more and more agency executive directors, I hear the same comments—donations are down, government budgets are being cut, the cost of operating services is increasing, and it is hard to balance an organizational budget. The giving environment that supports the helping of people is causing services to be reduced, or even shut down.

The non-profit community is forced to think outside of the box and respond to this threatening trend of decreasing resources. Two significant developments are occurring.

The first is "co-location" of services. More agencies need to co-locate their services onto one site in order to save overhead costs, and also integrate services with each other. If a community agency is going to rent or purchase one facility, why not locate dozens of agencies in that one building and share the costs? It just makes sense.

The second is "co-management" of agencies. Organizations need to develop strategic mergers—just like the corporate world—where agencies share management costs. Rather than five separate non-profit homeless service organizations hiring five CEO's, and five separate administrative, development, and finance staffs, why not hire one CEO and one management team to manage an alliance of five agencies?

Think of the savings that the service provider community would possess by sharing the cost of facilities and staff. Then let's challenge this community to invest this savings into building more permanent affordable housing.

There is hope.

Afterword

Homeless people are not "them" or "others" or even "criminals." They turn out to be you and me, and our friends, neighbors, and acquaintances.

They are our co-worker, who served in a war and turned to drugs or alcohol to cope with terrifying memories; our neighbor, who, after mental illness ravaged his ability to maintain a job, lost his family life; the waitress who, after finally escaping an abusive husband, still could not afford to feed her children. They are ordinary people stuck in extraordinary circumstances.

The man standing at the foot of the freeway off-ramp asking drivers for a handout makes us feel uncomfortable. We might give him some spare change, or ignore him and roll up the window, wave, or even say "I'm sorry." We might wonder how he got there, what separates him from us, seated in our comfortable automobiles, our bellies not aching for lack of food, and our lives waiting for us at home. Did we simply make better choices? Are we simply "luckier?" Or do we work harder for what we have, and he, by contrast, has opted out of life?

There is no universal solution to each of these folks' problems, and there is no single solution to the "homeless problem." There are many reasons why a person might be living on the streets, and often a long, winding road of explanation as to how they arrived there. Joel John Roberts explores these complex societal issues by asking the thought-provoking question, "Do we *want* to have homeless people in our society?"

Of course the logical, humane answer is "no," but Joel's examination of how our communities and how we as individuals deal with the homeless would seem to indicate otherwise. Why do we criminalize the homeless? Why are so many veterans swept aside by the very government and the people that they swore to protect? Why are the needs of the mentally ill ignored, or worse, judged in criminal courts?

The reason we are uncomfortable with homelessness is not because it is so removed from our lives; rather, it is because it represents the worst that can happen to people like us, to our loved ones, to "normal" people. There are more families than ever—including women and children— now living on the streets of America. How many families who have homes now are one or two paychecks away from being on the street?

The lack of housing that is affordable and decent is reaching a crisis point in our urban job centers and large-city suburbs. According to Harvard's Joint Center for Housing Studies 2004 "State of the Nation's Housing Report," more than twice as many people in the United States face housing dilemmas as lack health insurance.

This means there are growing numbers of people who are literally, *one paycheck away* from living on the street. The somber reality of the homeless population is that many are recently dispossessed by the economic hardship of trying to afford a decent home for themselves and their families.

Every homeless person has a special story, requiring a special solution. And the overwhelming, increasing numbers of homeless magnifies the need for solutions. In Los Angeles, for example, there are an estimated 80,000 or more homeless people living on the streets. One by one, People Assisting The Homeless (PATH) have been providing solutions with dignity and respect for these people, many of whom are women and children, for more than twenty years. Therein seems to lie the key to solving this crisis in our society: treating the homeless *person*, not the homeless *problem*.

PATH accomplishes this feat by providing many different services at its Los Angeles facility. Opened in 2002, the PATH Regional Homeless Center is a collaboration of nearly two dozen community and government social service agencies which form a "one-stop shopping center" for homeless individuals.

Each year, the 40,000 square foot PATH Mall transforms the lives of thousands: 1,200 people receive mental health assistance, 500 people find permanent employment, 850 people receive health care, and over 6,000 people receive free haircuts and manicures. The value of services like this is immeasurable. How can someone find the road back to a normal life, and look for work, if they are confused and ill, or have been living on the streets and in need of personal grooming?

Much more is needed than just a temporary bed and a meal to help a person transition from living on the street to having a steady job, a home and a productive life. Many of the dispossessed work hard to turn their lives around, only to collapse under the pressures of a normal life. The solutions need to be long-term; after years of being destitute, the structured demands of a normal life can be as unfamiliar to them as street life would be to you or I.

It takes a caring, expertly staffed system of management to deal with the crisis of homelessness. PATH is an example of what works. As Joel so effectively describes, the alternatives currently in practice do not. By taking the time to better understand the people who are homeless, perhaps we will better understand the many ways we as a society can help them.

— **G. Allan Kingston**

G. Allan Kingston is President/CEO of Century Housing, a nonprofit lender and an intermediary for the creation of affordable and workforce housing. He has directed Century's real estate financing and development programs since 1989 and has brought to reality Century's *More Than Shelter*® social amenities.

Century has financed more than 11,000 units of affordable housing in 120 developments, for more than 15,000 Southland families throughout the Los Angeles metropolitan area. Century's investments have created affordable housing worth over $200 million in 66 communities in the Los Angeles area.

Mr. Kingston provides national leadership in the movement to end homelessness, including:

- The Chairman of the Board of Governors of the National Housing Conference, the oldest national advocacy organization for the provision of affordable and workforce housing.

- The Chairman of the Board of Directors of the California Housing Consortium, an affiliate of the National Housing Conference and the only organization representing nonprofit and for-profit developers, lenders, representatives from state and local government agencies, housing professionals, united together in a nonpartisan effort to advance affordable housing and community development issues throughout California.

- Serves on the Boards of: the National Association of Affordable Housing Lenders, the National Housing Development Corporation, the Center for Housing Policy, Shelter Partnership of Los Angeles, Housing California, and the National Coalition for Homeless Veterans.

What is More Than Shelter?

More Than Shelter is the belief that quality of life starts *after* the walls and roof are placed on a home; social amenities, rather than physical amenities, make all the difference. Century Housing links the quality, affordable housing it has helped create with More Than Shelter social amenities, to build communities. Some examples of Century's successful More Than Shelter accomplishments include: Assisting in the development of 10 Child Development Centers, serving more than 700 children of low-income families; serving 2,000 low-income seniors annually with activity and wellness services through the More Than Shelter For Seniors program; monitoring the affordability of 3,600 Century-financed units; placing 1,000 men & women in construction trades through the Century Community Training Program; providing 458 "silent second" mortgage loans; counseling 1,500 households on homeownership responsibilities; and helping 26 families with homeownership down payment assistance.

APPENDIX A

People Assisting The Homeless

Increasing homelessness means more and more people are living on the streets. The result is a growing demand of homeless support services.

This is why all proceeds of this book will support the work of PATH (People Assisting The Homeless), a regional homeless service agency based in Los Angeles, California. For twenty years, this program has been providing services for people who are homeless, helping them overcome personal barriers, finding work, and accessing affordable housing.

PATH has become a trend-setting agency that is promoting a national model of integrated services based on co-location. The PATH Mall, located in the heart of Los Angeles, houses nearly two dozen public and private social service agencies. So a person who is homeless has access to nearly every service needed—employment training, substance abuse treatment, mental health care, public benefits, legal advice, etc.—all at one location. (See Chapter Ten, "Access Denied").

Every month in Los Angeles, PATH is serving nearly 2,000 people who are homeless. Nearly all of them are homeless as a result of at least one issue described in this book.

To learn more about PATH, visit www.epath.org.

Reader's Guide

Chapters One and Two: The Absurd

- Is the picture of our community described in these chapters realistic? Or is it sensationalized? How does it compare to your own community?

- Who is to blame for homelessness in our community?

- Our federal government provides one billion dollars each year for homeless services. Why do you think homelessness still persists when so much money is already invested? Would more money help or should funding be reduced?

- What do you think about the conclusion: Maybe we don't really want homelessness to end. Is it absurd? Could it actually be true? What do you think is the author's real reason for proposing such a conclusion?

Chapter Three: The Conspiracy

- Do you know how many homeless people are in your community, and how many shelter beds? If not, contact your local government office or social service agency to find out.

- How do you feel about the reasons listed for the proposed conspiracy? Is it silly? Could there be some truth?

- Do you think proposing an absurd conspiracy on increasing homelessness helps further the cause of ending homelessness? If so, how?

Chapter Four: Build Our House On Sand

- Find out what the average cost of rent for an apartment in your community is. Is it too high?

- Do you think the American Dream of owning your own home is more reachable now than it was perhaps twenty or thirty years ago? Or less reachable? And why?

- Why do you think gentrification (people who are well off moving into lower-income neighborhoods) has a negative stigma for some activists? If you were a person living in a poorer neighborhood, would you want higher-income people to move and renovate your community in order to raise the values of your neighborhood? How would that affect you?

Chapter Five: Keep Minimum Wage At A Minimum

- Create a fictional budget of living expenses in your community—rent, food, utilities, clothing, travel, etc. How does this compare to the federal minimum wage of $5.15 per hour? Can you live on minimum wage? As a single person, as a single parent with one child, as a parent with multiple children?

- If you were living on minimum wage, what things could you do to make ends meet and/or save money?

- Calculate what your local "living wage" might be—a wage that is high enough to be able to rent a local apartment and provide all of your necessities.

- Would you support a "living wage" ordinance in your community that would increase the minimum wage, even if it meant job losses? How would you justify reducing the number of jobs in a community in order to increase wages?

- Do you think our country should try to stop "outsourcing" jobs to other countries? Why or why not?

- How much money do you think a family should have socked away in a savings account in order to protect them from becoming homeless?

Chapter Six: No Free Lunch

- Do you think every community in America should have a law that provides a shelter bed for anyone who is homeless (like New York City)? How could a community or city pay for such a law?

- Do you think people should be required to work for their "free bed"? Why do people deserve free rent and board?

Chapter Seven: The Homeless Outlaw

- Should it be against the law to sleep, beg, and/or urinate in public? Or do you think that people have the civil right to sleep, beg, and/or urinate in public if there are not enough shelter beds or bathrooms in a community?

- How would you feel if the neighbor living across the street from your house let his yard and house become a total junkyard? Would you complain to the authorities? Cleaning up blight is the "broken windows" approach to bettering the community. Some people would include homelessness as one component of "blight" in a community. Read more about the "broken windows" approach by searching the internet, and decide if this approach is appropriate for your community.

- Do you think your community has enough homeless services to deal with the problem? Call your local city office and ask them how many services are in the community.

Chapter Eight: Don't Ask, Don't Plan

- Contact the programs in your community that may be contributing to the increase of homelessness (jails, mental health facilities, foster care, etc.) and ask them how they prevent their clients from becoming homeless.

- In difficult economic times, services are usually cut to balance budgets. That means more people are need of services, and less services are being offered. How would you resolve this social problem—balance a budget while still providing enough services for people in need?

Chapter Nine: The Leaf Blower Mentality

- Ask your local law enforcement agency what they do when the community complains about homeless people. Do they arrest the homeless people? Tell them to leave and go somewhere else? Or do nothing?

- How would you respond if a nearby town tells all the homeless people to go to your town because your town has a feeding program?

- When homelessness persists across a region, is it fair for only a handful of the local communities to solve the problem? How would you encourage all communities to respond together?

Chapter Ten: Access Denied

- Take a map and mark where all of the social service agencies are located in your community. Compare it to bus routes. How hard is it for a person to travel to each of these services? How long would it take? How much would it cost?

- What would be your ideal homeless service center? What types of services would you include in this facility? Where would you locate it in your community?

Chapter Eleven: Fostering Homelessness

- Imagine a young person being placed in one foster family after another before he turned 18 years old. What would you do to insure that he had the tools and motivation to continue on to college or to find a job and an apartment?

- In your life, who is your "village"—the group of people that surround you with care and encouragement? How do we provide such a "village" to young people who have been abandoned by their families?

Chapter Twelve: Eliminate Welfare

- How do you feel about the latest welfare reform legislation where people have access to public assistance for a maximum number of five years? Do you think it is working?

- How do you think our government should respond to welfare "cheaters," those people who don't truly need government assistance but still receive it?

- How would you compare corporate government entitlements to personal welfare assistance?

- How does a government financially help its people living in poverty without creating people who become dependent on the government?

Chapter Thirteen: Bring On The War

- Do you agree with the author that there is a correlation between military service and becoming homeless? Why?

- If Post-Traumatic Stress Disorder is a side-affect of war, how can our government protect veterans leaving their tour of duty from this disorder? How can we prepare families who receive their veteran spouses and parents back?

Chapter Fourteen: Free Will For The Mentally Ill

- How do we balance the civil rights of a person struggling with mental illness and the rights of a community to be safe and secure?

- Should we be able to incarcerate a mentally disturbed person without that person's permission? What circumstances do you think are appropriate in order to allow forced incarceration?

Chapter Fifteen: At The Trough

- How do we feed hungry people, without having them become dependent on us? How do we teach them how to "fish"?

- If we do allow groups to feed the hungry and homeless on public property, should a community place restrictions on the program? (Limit the hours, clean eating and cooking facilities, limit the location, etc.)

- Do you think direct mail pieces and newspaper display ads that use hungry people to appeal for donations is appropriate? Furthers the cause of ending homelessness?

Chapter Sixteen: NIMBYs R Us

- Would you vote to allow a homeless shelter to move onto your neighborhood block? Why or why not?

- Do you think there is a correlation between the location of homeless programs and the increase of homeless people loitering at that location? If so, why?

- If no community wants to house homeless programs, then what do we do?

- How do you feel about an Inclusionary Zoning Ordinance where every community would have to bear the burden of housing service programs?

Chapter Seventeen: Bootstraps In An Age of Sneakers

- What percentage of people who are homeless do you think are just lazy?

- Should we expect the same success from a young teenage boy who grows up in an environment of books and calculators as a young teenager who grows up in a neighborhood filled with guns and drugs?

Chapter Eighteen: Give Them Liberty, Not Death

- How would you answer this question from a foreign visitor? "How can the richest country in the world allow its people to live in such abject poverty on the streets?"

- Is it appropriate for a country to give a citizen the right to live in extreme poverty, especially if the country has the resources to help? Why?

- What percentage of people who are homeless do you think choose to be homeless?

Chapter Nineteen: Give It Up

- It is true that some people end up homeless because they have given up on life? Do you think our community has given up on helping them? Why?

- How do you respond when you see that television, newspaper, or mail solicitation on feeding the hungry or helping the homeless? Are you skeptical that it's just another scam? Tired of the constant asking? Compassionate to give again?

- What motivates you to give to an organization that helps the hungry or needy?

- When you think of the homeless problem are you: Angry? Anxious? Apathetic? Action-oriented? Why?

Chapter Twenty: An Extreme Machine

- Do you think the idea of "Can't we all just get along?" is an unreachable dream? Or will we always have conflict in our community?

- Why do the "loud" extreme groups, with extreme opinions seem to dominate the discussion on homelessness?

- What groups in the community could become mediators that could silence the shouts and finger-pointing and actually facilitate solutions?

Chapter Twenty-One: Imagine

- Who could be the prophets in our community who would be willing to stand up to the decision-makers and stalwarts and express the concern to help the homeless?

- How can we project positive images of a community free of homelessness?

Chapter Twenty-Two: Hunting For Good Will

- If there is a will there is a way. Do you think your community has the political will to solve homelessness? Why?

- What tangible ways can a community instill political will toward ending homelessness?

About the Author

Joel John Roberts is the CEO and Executive Director of the The PATH Partners that includes People Assisting The Homeless, Project New Hope, Homestead Hospices, PATH Ventures and CONNECTIONS.

For nearly eight years, he has directed PATH, a trend-setting homeless agency, developing it into a national model of integrated services. He led the team that developed the PATH Mall, a center that houses nearly two dozen public and private social service agencies all based at one site. This unique "one-stop" center has become a model for hundreds of communities nationally and internationally. It has been highlighted on ABC World News Tonight, British Broadcasting Corporation, National Public Radio and numerous local media outlets.

Roberts has been active on the local and state level in combating homelessness. He is a former chairman of the Los Angeles Homeless Services Authority Advisory Board, board member of the Westside Hunger and Shelter Coalition, member of the L.A. County Sheriff's Caucus for the Homeless and the L.A. Mayor's Blue Ribbon Panel on Homelessness, panelist for the California Governor's Homeless Summit, Advisory Board member of the Asian Pacific AIDS Intervention Team, and a Zero Divide Fellow of the Community Technology Foundation of California.

He earned a Bachelor's Degree in Communications at California State University of Long Beach and a Master's Degree in Cross-Cultural Studies at Fuller Seminary.

Roberts was an orphan in Asia, born in Hong Kong, until he was adopted into a family in Long Beach, California when he was two years old. His family provided all of the same tools of success—love, education, hope, and faith—that he seeks to instill in those that are being served at PATH.

Roberts lives in Santa Monica, California with two of his three children. His third child is an adult living in Long Beach. He has written several op-ed pieces for the Los Angeles Times and the California Real Estate Journal, and has been featured in several local and national television news segments.